4. 1.8 bc

THE 250 QUESTIONS
EVERY
HOMEBUYER
SHOULD ASK

Christie Craig

Adams Media
Avon, Massachusetts

Copyright ©2005, F+W Publications, Inc.
All rights reserved. This book, or parts thereof, may not be
reproduced in any form without permission from the publisher;
exceptions are made for brief excerpts used in published reviews.

Published by
Adams Media, an F+W Publications Company
57 Littlefield Street, Avon, MA 02322. U.S.A.
www.adamsmedia.com

ISBN: 1-59337-265-5

Printed in Canada.

J   I   H   G   F   E   D   C   B   A

Library of Congress Cataloging-in-Publication Data
Craig, Christie.
The 250 questions every homebuyer should ask / Christie Craig.
p.   cm.
ISBN 1-59337-265-5
1. House buying—Miscellanea. I. Title: The two hundred fifty
questions every homebuyer should ask. II. Title.
HD1379.C73 2005
643'.12—dc22
2004013573

This publication is designed to provide accurate and authoritative information
with regard to the subject matter covered. It is sold with the understanding
that the publisher is not engaged in rendering legal, accounting, or other professional advice. If legal advice or other expert assistance is required, the services of a competent professional person should be sought.
—From a *Declaration of Principles* jointly adopted by a Committee of the
American Bar Association and a Committee of Publishers and Associations

Many of the designations used by manufacturers and sellers to distinguish
their products are claimed as trademarks. Where those designations appear in
this book and Adams Media was aware of a trademark claim, the designations
have been printed with initial capital letters.

This book is available at quantity discounts for bulk purchases.
For information, please call 1-800-872-5627.

Contents

Part One

Deciding to Purchase ... 1

This section covers questions frequently asked by consumers as they first begin to contemplate buying a home: Buying versus Renting, Where to Get the Money for a Down Payment, Where Do You Want to Live?, Affording a Home, Real Estate Agents, Credit Issues.

Part Two

Loan Wisdom ... 55

This section covers the ins and outs of loans: Deciding on the Right Loan, Applying for a Loan, Fixed Rates versus ARMs, FHA Loans, VA Loans, How to Compare Lenders, Loans with Low Down Payments.

Part Three

Shopping for a Home ... 105

This section covers questions about shopping for a home: Checking Out a Neighborhood, Should You Consider a Fixer-Upper?, What are the Most Common Defects of an Older Home?, Disclosures, Questions You Need to Ask about the Homeowners Association, New Homes versus Older Homes.

Part Four

Making an Offer ... 133

This section includes everything you need to know about making an offer: Purchasing Agreements, Contingencies, Deciding a Home's Value, Negotiating Tips, Insurance Questions, Counter-offers, Inspections.

Part Five

Closing and Contract Facts ... 157

In this section you will find information on the closing and basic contract information that will get you through the last step of the homebuying process: Closing Costs, Title Insurance, Loan Fees, Fees to Watch Out for, Closing Day Tasks.

Acknowledgments

I would like to thank several people for their support while I harvested the information to bring this book to completion: my husband, Steve Craig, who in all rights should be cowriter for his in-depth research; my son, Steven Craig, who ate frozen dinners and never complained; Nita Craft and Francyne Anderson, who gave me whining rights and understood when I missed lunch dates to make the deadline; Teri Thackston, my critique partner and friend, whose keen eye caught many mistakes and whose encouraging words were worth gold; my agent, Mary Sue Seymour, who sold me on the project; my editor, Danielle Chiotti, who also gave me whining rights and was there when I had inquiries; and last, but not least, Phil Allan, my real estate agent, who never tired of my countless questions, which probably equaled more than 250.

Introduction

B uying a home is an exhilarating experience that can be both wonderful and mind boggling. The decision to purchase isn't just one big step, it is a process of steps leading up to a giant leap into the world of real estate investing. As with all giant leaps in life, the trick to buying a home is to arm oneself with enough knowledge that the huge undertaking doesn't feel so huge or scary.

There are five sections in this book, each one written to get you through the various stages of homebuying. From that very beginning point of asking yourself if buying is right for you to that final moment when the keys to your new home are pressed into your palm, this book will guide you through steps A to Z.

The goal of *250 Questions Every Homebuyer Should Ask* is to help make this experience a lot more wonderful and a lot less mind boggling.

Part One

Deciding to Purchase

You have been contemplating buying a home. But where do you start? How do you know if you're ready? You probably have plenty of questions—and that's a good thing. Buying a home is a huge undertaking, one that deserves to be thought through carefully.

This section will help you prepare as you make those first steps toward becoming a homeowner. It will take you through the pros and cons of buying versus renting, deciding on the type of home you want, and choosing the right real estate agent.

Q: To own or rent—which is right for you?

A: While most Americans own their own homes, this isn't to say that homeownership is for everyone. If you have credit problems, if you move frequently, or if you simply do not want the responsibility of owning a home, then renting might be a better option.

Pros of Renting

People who choose to rent over buying will quickly point out the advantages of renting. Some of these advantages are:

- When renting or leasing, the landlord or owner of the property will most likely be responsible for the cost of any work or repairs that are done to the property.
- Generally, you need less cash up front to move into a rental property.
- Because most rental properties are apartment dwellings, you will not spend your weekends mowing the lawn or trimming the hedges.

Cons of Renting

While the advantages of renting do exist, this isn't to say there aren't a few negatives.

- Renting is not always the best way to maximize your investments. You have none of the tax advantages of a property owner.
- If you don't live in a rent-controlled space, your monthly payments can be unpredictable from lease to lease.
- Renting means that you normally can't change the color of the walls or the carpet to suit your taste. In

many ways, renting is a little like living under someone else's house rules.

■ Renting, especially in apartments, can bring a lot
of parking issues. You may be limited to only one
parking space.

Pros of Owning

Depending on your lifestyle and your preferences, buying
may be a better option for you. Take a look at some of the
pros of buying/owning a home:

■ Purchasing a home is generally a sound investment,
as it increases in value over time.

■ Purchasing a home will give you the benefit of tax
advantages. The mortgage interest and real estate
taxes are tax deductible, meaning you can subtract
part of your housing-related expenses from your
income, thereby reducing your tax liability.

■ Home is where the heart is! Owning your own home
means the freedom to make decisions—remodeling
to suit your own tastes, being a permanent part of a
community, deciding if you'd like to have a pet.

Cons of Owning

In spite of all the advantages of buying a home, a homebuyer
must weigh both the financial risks and responsibilities.

■ Today's financial experts are saying that Americans
are buying more house than they need and can afford.
The square footage of an average home has almost
doubled in size from those built in the 1950s.

■ Look closely at your lifestyle and your finances to make
sure that homeowning is the best option for you.

Q: Can I afford to buy a home?

A: To many, buying a home is part of the American dream. Yet, only by being aware of all your financial responsibilities and needs can you be assured that your dream will meet your expectations. Be sure to research thoroughly, and to ask the right questions.

> **Homebuying Myth:** "I can afford a home if my house payments are comparable to my monthly rent."
>
> **Homebuying Fact:** While this may seem like a fair judgment, the reality is that there is often a significant increase in living costs once you own your home. Think of it like paying on a car. There's much more to it than just a monthly payment. There are also gas, insurance, tags, maintenance, and more.

It's the same thing with buying a home—depending on the size of the home, your utilities can increase as much as 50 percent. There are the costs of insurance, taxes, fees for homeowners associations, the price of furnishing the new home, the upkeep, decorating costs, and don't forget the 20 percent down payment.

Are You Ready? Questions to Ask Yourself

Only by carefully assessing your financial picture and considering the increase in living costs can you truly know if you can afford to purchase a home. Consulting a financial advisor or someone you trust to help review your financial situation is a wise decision. Another way to know if you can afford a home is to get prequalified for a loan.

In addition, questions such as those below might give you insight into your readiness for making this big purchase:

- Do you have a source of income? Have you been employed on a regular basis for the last few years? Is your current income a reliable source?
- Do you have very few outstanding long-term debts such as a car loan or school loans?
- Do you have a good record of paying bills on time?
- Do you have money saved or available for a down payment?
- Do you have the ability to make a mortgage payment, plus the additional costs of homeownership?
- Have you really investigated all the costs and responsibilities of owning a home?

If you can answer yes to all or most of these questions, you may be ready to take the plunge into homeowning. It is wise to remember that, even if your monetary resources can't withstand a mortgage now, planning and budgeting can help prepare you for the purchase in the future.

Q: How much can I afford?

A: Generally speaking, most people can afford a home that is worth about three times their total (gross) annual income. If you make an annual income of $50,000, you can probably afford a home around $150,000. This is estimated assuming that the homebuyer has made a 20 percent down payment and has an average amount of other long-term debts such as a car loan, school loans, or credit card bills.

Get Prequalified
If you have very low or no debt, you can probably afford a house valued up to four or five times your annual income.

If you're unsure as to how much you can afford, consider getting prequalified for a loan. Just keep in mind that loan officers are trained to look at numbers and may not understand your personal needs. It's smart to take a serious look at where your money is spent now. Do you spend a larger than average amount on entertainment? Are you into buying the latest and greatest electronic equipment or expensive cars? Are these things essential to your happiness? If the answer is yes, be sure to budget them into the overall picture. It is important to remember that the pride of owning a home can be squelched if the quality of your life has been sacrificed beyond the point you are willing to give.

Q: How much money will I need to buy a house?

A: Of course, the answer to this question will depend on numerous variables—from the cost of the home to the type of down-payment requirements connected to your loan. But on average, you'll need 10 to 20 percent of the cost of the home for a down payment. On top of the down-payment expense, you can expect to pay approximately 4 to 6 percent on closing costs. So let's say you're looking at purchasing a home for approximately $100,000. You would need anywhere from $10,000 to $20,000 for the down payment, and closing costs could fall between $4,000 and $6,000. Worst case scenario, you might need $26,000.

If it sounds like a lot of money, it is. However, you should remember, that is the worst case scenario and there are all sorts of loan options and government programs that will allow you a lower down payment. (See the "Loan Wisdom" section for specific information on loans that offer lower down-payment options.)

Q: How can I begin to budget for buying a house?

A: Does the word budget sends chills of fear running down your spine? You're not alone. This is possibly the largest purchase you'll make in your life. While a little worrying is perfectly natural, preparing and setting a budget isn't just smart—it's necessary.

Basic Budget Guidelines

In order to create a budget, you must take account of all of your monthly income. Look at your basic needs—food, shelter, and bills—and deduct those expenses from your total dollar amount. How much do you have left? What are your other expenses? Do you know where your money is really going each month?

Many financial advisers recommend that, when planning your budget, you keep a record, for at least one month, of every dime you spend. (A small notebook kept in your purse or back pocket can easily be used to keep track of this information.) Many people are surprised to discover that their soda and candy bar attacks, or their drive-by coffee breaks, are costing them hundreds of dollars a month. Eating out and entertainment are one area many want-to-be home-owners find themselves having to cut back on to start their down-payment savings.

Cutting Back

After you seriously account for where your money is going, ask yourself how much you are willing to sacrifice for the pleasure of owning your own home. Can you cut back on the grocery bill by clipping coupons? Can you get a library card instead of spending the money you normally do on books? Are you really going to the gym or just paying the fifty dollars on monthly membership fees in hopes that next month you'll find more time? It is crucial to set a budget you can follow. Planning a budget is often compared to starting a diet. You can't deprive yourself of everything you enjoy and not expect to fall off the bandwagon. If you leave yourself no wiggle room or entertainment funds, you may give in to temptation, and throw the budget out the window.

By being creative, reasonable, and sticking with a budget plan, you can watch your savings start to grow. If you have a family, get them involved. Have meetings and report the savings—ask for other money-saving suggestions. Perhaps keep a record of the savings on the refrigerator to help you stay motivated. If you have children, this is a great life lesson. For help in setting a budget, and other financial advice, check out *www.daveramsey.com.*

Q: Saving sounds great, but it would take years—am I the only person who doesn't have an extra $10,000 or $15,000 at my disposal to use as a down payment?

A: No, you are not alone. There are many cases when saving for the down payment just isn't feasible. In addition, if it took you years to save the down payment, home prices are going to be climbing. Depending on your discretionary income, you may have to look at alternative sources. In the "Loan Wisdom" section, you will find a variety of loan options and government programs. However, for now, let's look at how most Americans manage to pull together a down payment for a home.

Down-Payment Options

According to the National Association of Realtors Profile of Home Buyers and Sellers, 22 percent of first-time buyers depended on gifts from relatives or friends to pay for their down payments. Looking to your parents for a "leg up" into the world of homeowning isn't uncommon. If you are fortunate enough to have help, be aware that your lender will want to verify where your initial down payment has come from. If the money was a gift, the lender will want to see check stubs or a letter from your parents (or whoever has given the money to you) indicating that the financial resource was, in fact, a gift. Also be aware that gifts over $10,000 may incur additional taxes from the IRS.

Private loans are also a way to get into your dream home. However, be aware that most financial advisers are not too keen on recommending borrowing from family and friends. Too many good relationships have been hurt due to monetary reasons. If you do choose to go this route, make sure you discuss all expectations of when and how the loan will be repaid and put the details in writing.

On an average, 57 percent of repeat buyers acquired their down payment from the equity from a previous home. If this is your first home, even if you don't have family or friends able to help, don't give up without first looking closely at your other resources.

Are you sitting on cash that you haven't considered? Do you have stocks you can sell? Do you have a life insurance policy you can borrow against? Do you have personal items like a boat, RV, jewelry, or an extra car that you could sell?

In your eagerness to acquire the extra cash, be careful not to leave yourself short of emergency resources. And before you start selling off Grandma's silver or other things that have sentimental value, check into your loan options that offer lower down payments.

If you decide to liquidate assets (sell those items for cash), it is best to get the money into a savings account as fast as possible. Don't wait until two days before you need the down payment to sell the pair of diamond earrings you've decided you could live without.

Q: Can I use any of the funds in my IRA for the down payment?

A: Yes. Thanks to the 1997 Taxpayer Relief Act, first-time homebuyers can withdraw up to $10,000 penalty-free from their individual retirement account (IRA) for a down payment to purchase a home. While there is no penalty, you may have to pay income tax on the amount drawn. Check with your tax accountant or the IRS about rules for IRA withdrawals. To review the IRA rules, go to *www.irs.gov.*

Several conditions are contingent to the IRA withdrawal offer. The $10,000 amount is a lifetime limit. The money must be used within 120 days of the date you receive it. Also, the offer is open only to those who are considered first-time homeowners. If a couple is buying a home together, both parties must qualify as first-time buyers. The good news is that the law defines a first-time homeowner as someone who hasn't owned a house for the past two years.

Q: Can I use any of the funds in my 401K for the down payment?

A: According to the 2000 National Association of Realtors Profile of Home Buyers and Sellers, 4 to 5 percent of homebuyers took loans out against their 401K to be able to afford their down payments.

In general, if you are participating in your employer's tax-deferred retirement plan, you can borrow up to a specified limit from the account penalty-free to buy a house. A relative who participates can also draw from his or her account to help you purchase a home. If it is your account, because you do have to repay the money, it will be viewed by the lender as outstanding debt and calculated into your income-to-debt ratio.

The conditions of the 401K loans are set by your employer. Each company may have different minimum loan amounts, interest rates, and loan fees. The tax code states that the loan must be repaid in a "reasonable amount of time," however they do not define reasonable.

On a last note, it is wise to find out what happens if you leave your job before fully repaying a loan from your 401K. The loan may become due immediately on departure and tax penalties may apply to the outstanding balance.

Q: What type of house do I want and need?

A: Once you have an idea of what you can afford, it's time to focus on what your desires and necessities are in a home. Are you in the market for a condominium or a single-family detached home? Are you set on a new home, a used home with few or no needed repairs, or a fixer-upper?

List Your Priorities
You may already have a vision in your head of the perfect home, or perhaps you're just now ready to start seriously considering your wants and needs. Either way, it's good to sharpen your pencil and start making a list of your priorities.

The list should consist of the type of home, the style, overall size, room sizes, location, type of neighborhood, and choice of flooring and windows. A good way to begin your list is to remember past residences. Recall as best you can the things you disliked: small closets, not enough windows, tiny bathrooms, bad neighborhood. On the flip side, it's important to recall the things you liked about a home: the French doors leading into a large backyard, a yard with lots of trees, a covered patio, a large kitchen with an island, a master bedroom with a fireplace. Other ways to jumpstart your list are visiting model homes, driving through neighborhoods, and flipping through home magazines. As you window shop, take note of the homes that catch your eye, that cause you to stop and pause. We seldom get everything we want, but if you know what you like, your chances of getting a home that fits your lifestyle are much better.

Consider Life Changes

While compiling your priority list, consider any upcoming changes in your life that may alter your needs. Are you planning a family or about to become empty nesters? Do you have aging parents you plan to care for? Do you plan someday soon to start working out of your home? If so, wouldn't it be smart to buy a property that has a large basement or garage? And if this is the case, don't forget to make sure the zoning of the property will allow you to conduct business. After completing the list, prioritize the wants and the needs. Is it more important to have the fourth bedroom, or to have the upstairs game room? Is the large backyard more important than the third bathroom?

Now consider how the priorities might change if you had to settle for only ten items on your list. Could you hone it down to five? It is important to remember that first-time buyers are simply getting into the market, therefore your true dream house may be two or three houses in the future. Yet, knowing your top requirements and being able to communicate them to a real estate agent are essential to finding a place you'll be proud to call home.

Q: Where do I want to live?

A: Most people have fantasies of their perfect home and where the dream house is located. To some, a ranch-style home on ten acres in the country, room for a few horses, and maybe a barn with a rooster thrown in for the quaint effect, is the ideal. Others want a three-bedroom, two-bath home with a white picket fence in a suburban neighborhood. There are those who dream of inner-city dwellings with art galleries and a theater within a stone's throw. A person's lifestyle generally plays a big part in their preferences. However, lifestyle isn't the only thing that designates where a person chooses to live.

It is extremely important to know everything there is to know about the state, city, and neighborhood where you are purchasing your home. Be aware of your lifestyle preferences and those of your family as you look at your options. If you or your spouse are considering changing careers or are just now graduating from college, look at the career opportunities in the town/city you've chosen to purchase property in.

Included in this book are questions about the pros and cons of inner city, country, and suburban living. You'll find more in-depth questions on how to evaluate a location's living conditions in the "Shopping for a Home" section of this book.

When you are in the beginning stages of considering a home purchase, narrowing the focus of what you want will save you and your agent lots of legwork and frustration. This isn't to say that you shouldn't look into different options, but basically, some questions of your wants, needs, desires, and expectations should be answered early on.

If you are moving to a new state, even a bordering town, or if your move is going to take you into a new way of life, such as a move from the city to a rural area, the best piece of advice anyone can give you is to lease or rent a place for six months to a year before buying. No amount of research on a location will give you the insight and experience that living in a place can bring.

Below are some more points that everyone needs to think about before deciding on a location.

Commuting Time

Whether it's the city, suburbs, or a rural area, the commuting time is a primary factor that needs to be investigated. Living twenty miles from your work doesn't sound so bad, but in some places, twenty miles can translate to a two-hour drive one way during peak traffic times. While going back and forth to work is the main "commuting concern," consider other travel times as well. How long is it to a local grocery store or to the closest movie theater? In some instances a move can negate your need for a car or require the purchase of one.

Schools

If you have children, or are thinking of having children, it is crucial that you investigate the school system before buying. Know how the schools rate, where they are located, and if they offer a bus system with which you are comfortable. You would be surprised how many people regret their home purchase or move due to schools. (See page 107 on how to check out a school system.)

Health Concerns

Are you, or is someone in your family, older or do you have health concerns? Consider how close you need to be to local doctors or hospitals. Do you or someone in your family suffer from severe allergies? Should you check with your doctor before moving somewhere with a different climate or change in air quality?

Job Requirements for Resident Statuses

If you live in a city and hold a city job, you may be required by law to reside within those metropolitan borders. In addition, many regional government entities may have residency requirements.

Q: What are the advantages and disadvantages of living in the inner city?

A: With the many government grants and programs helping to rebuild our downtown areas, our inner cities are becoming more and more livable. Cities such as Houston—the fourth largest city in the United States—have seen an influx of growth in downtown residents unlike anything since pre–World War II days. It is even predicted that the population of downtown Houston will triple by 2010.

City dwellers at heart across the United States are finding the new urban living trend to be a long-awaited change. Those who love the vibrancy of a happening place have a list of advantages of inner-city living. Many city dwellers also work downtown, practically alleviating the issue of commuting. With public transportation generally available, many city residents feel as if a car is no longer needed. Those who live in the downtown areas are generally the people who want to feel as if they are in the hub of things. They enjoy knowing they are surrounded by culture, the museums, the galleries, and the theaters.

Oddly enough, what some people see as advantages, others see as disadvantages. Being in the hub of things generally means crowds, congestion, and noise. And while not having to own a car can be a plus to some, for city dwellers who aren't ready to give up their automobiles, things such as traffic and parking issues can be problematic.

Other things to consider when looking at property in the inner city are the crime rates and the school systems. While many states have reduced the inner-city crime rate, generally speaking, crime rates tend to be an issue for many homebuyers looking at city properties. And while there are some excellent city schools, on a whole, the suburban schools seem to hold popular appeal, with a larger percentage of inner-city children attending private schools than in the suburbs.

Q: What are the advantages and disadvantages of living in the suburbs?

A: Since suburban living came into being, it's been marketed as "a great place to raise a family," with backyards containing swing sets and a shaggy dog. Suburban living seems to imply neighbors that share similar lifestyles, affordable living, local parks, convenient shopping avenues, low crime rates, and good schools. And while some suburbs live up to consumers' expectations, it is up to individual homebuyers to know exactly what they are buying into. Wherever you go, you should investigate because crime rates vary from one suburb to another, property prices vary, and some school systems rate higher than others. (More information about evaluating neighborhoods, crime rates, and school systems can be found in the "Shopping for a Home" section of the book.)

While the suburbs may have been marketed to consumers with families, this isn't to say that some of the same advantages—affordable homes, lower crime rates, and convenient shopping—don't appeal to singles. Many singles adapt very well to the suburbs.

As for the disadvantages of suburban living, for many people who work in the city, it's the commute. Some homeowners who were drawn to the suburbs for family reasons find that the commute time away from their families overshadows the advantages of living in the suburbs.

An increasingly heard complaint of suburbanites regards the fees and regulations of homeowners associations tied to many subdivisions. Before buying into a neighborhood, it is important to know and understand all the homeowners association's requirements. (For more information on how to evaluate homeowners associations, see pages 114–115.)

Q: What are the advantages and disadvantages of living in the country?

A: There is no denying the appeal of rural life—nature, green pastures, rocking chairs on front porches where you can watch the sun set without even one high-rise building obstructing the view. The slower pace of country living is considered one of the biggest draws to living in a rural community. And yet what draws one person to the country can also be what drives another crazy. Some people just need to live in a place where something is always happening. And just as commuting to and from work can be a problem in the suburbs, it is one of the common complaints of rural residents.

Job opportunities are fewer in rural areas, and travel time to and from doctors, grocery stores, social clubs, restaurants, and so forth needs to be considered by those thinking about purchasing property away from the city and the convenience of the suburbs. While some parents see rural living as advantageous for raising well-balanced children, others consider rural schools lacking. Because no two areas are the same, the only way to know for sure what you can expect from a location regarding its school system, the crime rate, and the quality of life it provides is to do your own extensive investigation. The thing to remember is that every place comes with pros and cons, and only by weighing your options, understanding all the advantages and disadvantages, can you assure yourself that you'll be happy with a chosen location.

Q: What is a seller's market and a buyer's market?

A: Seller's market means that there are more buyers than sellers, and sellers can raise their prices and be very selective on the terms of a deal. You can recognize a seller's market by the average of how long houses stay on the market. When there is a low inventory of homes and they sell within thirty days, it is generally considered a seller's market. If possible, you may consider waiting a few months to see if there is a change.

A buyer's market is the flip side of the coin. Homes are not selling, the selection of homes is vast, and the smart seller will be willing to work with a homebuyer to secure a sale. So, as you can see, a buyer's market is what you want when you are shopping for a home. This isn't to say that it is impossible to get a good deal in a seller's market, but you will have to work faster and be prepared to pay a little more. Below are five tips for finding a home in a tight market:

- Visit homes as quickly as they come on the market.
- Stay in constant touch with your agent if you have one and be willing to juggle your schedule to visit new homes.
- Take a second look at the homes you rejected in case you missed some potential that may make the home acceptable.
- Be ready to make an offer quickly if you like the home.
- Do not be intimidated by multiple offers.

Q: Is there an optimum time of the year to shop for a home?

A: Generally speaking, more houses are on the market from April to September, due to the desire not to move children from one school district to another during a school year. Therefore, your selection of homes will be better during this peak season. In addition, the more homes available, the more likely sellers will be willing to lower their prices to compete in a competitive market. That said, as America's baby boomers are aging, more and more sellers are empty nesters, no longer worrying about school-age children; so the availability of homes during the summer season is lessoning, making buying a home less of a seasonal occurrence.

Q: Do I need a real estate agent?

A: A better question might be, "Why not use an agent?" A real estate agent can be an invaluable resource to you as you search for a home. A real estate agent can help you focus your search and analyze the market, will set up appointments for you to view prospective homes, and will accompany you on the visit. In addition, they will coordinate all aspects of the transaction, from presenting the offer to arranging inspections on the property. An agent will also help negotiate your purchase and basically will be there to answer any questions you may have. If you have inquiries about the area, the agent is again the person who can either answer your questions or lead you to someone who can. What does all this assistance cost you? Nothing. Unless you have hired an agent, more commonly called a buyer's broker, you don't pay for the agent's services. The seller does. (See pages 32–34 for more information on a buyer's broker.)

Q: How do I find a real estate agent?

A: While there are plenty of agents out there, it's important to find a knowledgeable agent who is a good match for you and your needs.

Take your time with this—interview several agents before deciding on one. When choosing an agent, ask yourself if you really feel comfortable with this person. Remember, not only will you and your family be spending lots of time with this person, but you will be sharing personal information with him or her about your finances, dreams, and goals.

The optimum way to locate the right agent is through personal referral. Talk to friends, neighbors, and coworkers to see if any of them recommend their agents. Agents, hoping for return business, sometimes keep in touch with their clients, so even acquaintances who haven't sold a house in the last few years may still have contacts. It's still good to remember that even an agent who comes highly recommended may not be the right agent for you. Some personalities just don't mesh. While you don't have to love everything about your agent, you will be spending a lot of time together as you search for the perfect home. Finding someone you can work with is important. Finding someone you can work with who is also good at his or her job can be tricky.

Aside from personal referrals, check your local papers, or papers in the town to which you're relocating, to find real estate agents. Look for the larger ads, for these are often placed by real estate offices as a reward for an agent's past success.

Q: How do I know if the real estate agent is qualified?

A: It is recommended that you first make sure your agent is a Realtor. A real estate agent is a Realtor when he or she becomes a member of the National Association of Realtors, the world's largest professional association. The word Realtor is a registered collective membership mark that identifies a real estate professional who is a member of the association and agrees to follow a strict code of ethics. Being part of an association doesn't mean someone is good at his or her job, but it does hold people to certain standards that are needed in business.

The agent you choose to work with should ideally:

- Be a full-time agent
- Have experience with the type of services you require

- Show integrity in his or her work
- Be a local resident
- Be a good communicator
- Be accessible and reliable
- Be sensitive to your tastes and needs

When you speak to an agent, be professional and organized. While you may not be the one writing out their check, it is by providing you with a service that they achieve success and an income.

Be assertive with your questions. Ask about the agent's credentials, experience, and common mode of practice. Does he or she work on weekends and evenings? How often should you expect to hear from her? What are her normal business hours? Does the agent have a reputation as one who closes on a lot of homes? A high-profile agent may help you purchase a home faster. On the other hand, an agent who closes on fewer homes may have more time to spend with you. By knowing what you want and expect, you can better select an agent who will meet your needs.

As you interview agents, make sure you take notes about their answers. Think carefully about the impressions you get from them. Do they seem to want to rush the interview? If so, consider the possibility they may not have time to help you search for the perfect home. Are they patient with your questions and do they explain things in simple terms without using real-estate jargon that leaves you feeling confused and intimidated?

A final piece of advice: always ask for references. Recent homebuyers will usually offer you an honest opinion of how they feel their agent performed. Many times, it will be a piece of information from a reference that will help you make your final decision.

Q: What is a multiple listing service?

A: A multiple listing service is a list of nearly all properties for sale in a given community. The lists are arranged by price and include pictures and all the important sales information. Glancing through the multiple listing is a good way to start your search for a home. This service is provided, for a cost, to real estate companies. Most agencies belong to a multiple listing service; however, some smaller agencies may not.

Q: Is one agency better than another?

A: While certain agencies do come with reputations due to the quality of agents they sign on to represent them, for the most part, agents are independent contractors. The agencies are simply a place to hang their licenses, and it is through the agencies' broker's license that agents are able to conduct business. Judging an agent by his or her agency is like judging a hair stylist by the salon where she works. The quality of your service will depend almost entirely on the agent and not the agency. That said, it never hurts to know the reputation of the agency. As with evaluating agents, personal references are always best. It doesn't hurt, however, to ask the agencies how they differ from some of their competitors. If a person is happy where he or she works and with the policies of his or her office, that person will generally do a better job. You could also check with the Better Business Bureau to make sure there haven't been any complaints against the agency.

When selling a home, the benefits the agency offers its agents and their clients, such as advertising specials, is more important to the client. One requirement a homebuyer will want the agency to provide is access to the multiple listing service (MLS).

Q: If the seller pays the fee of the agent, who does the agent really represent?

A: In most instances, when you start to work with an agent, you enter the relationship with only a handshake deal, never really understanding who the agent truly represents. Because handshake deals often leave unanswered questions on the conditions of the agreement, some states now require listing agents to offer clients a buyer representation agreement. Such contracts should detail where the agent's loyalties lie.

If you are not offered this information up front, ask. Don't be surprised by the answer. In most states, it is still common for an agent to be representing the seller and not the buyer. Real estate laws differ from state to state, and it's good to familiarize yourself with what you can expect. Many state agencies that regulate real estate agents have Web sites. To get more information on the regulatory agency in your state and to learn more about real estate laws and regulations, see U.S. State Resources on FindLaw at *www.findlaw.com/11stategov*. Start by looking at your state's home page for the state real estate department or commission.

Q: Do I need more than one agent?

A: Unless you are looking for homes in multiple towns, the answer is a firm no. Just as you assume the agent will be loyal to you, he or she has the same expectations. Even if you have entered the relationship with only a handshake and haven't signed contracts, there could be legal ramifications. For example, if you are shown a property by one agent and, for whatever reason, are not interested in the home, but another agent presents the property to you later and you decide to make an offer, both agents may feel they are entitled to a part of the commission. If the problem cannot be settled between all parties, it could result in a lawsuit, and the court time could delay a sale.

Some homebuyers feel they will see more homes if they work with more than one agent. However, with the multiple listing service, your agent should be able to link you up with any home in the area. This doesn't mean that you shouldn't be a part of the search. Comb through the real estate section of the newspaper, continue to drive through the neighborhoods where you would like to live. If you run across a property that is listed by a different agent, even if the property isn't posted on a multiple listing service, tell your agent and he or she can find out more about it.

Q: What does the term dual agency mean, and why isn't it recommended?

A: When the agent represents both the seller and the buyer, the transaction is called dual agency. Dual agency is very lucrative for real estate agents, since a single agent working both sides of the transaction collects the commission that would have normally been split between the buyer's agent and the seller's agent after closing. While this practice is illegal in some states, other states consider dual agency legal as long as both parties are disclosed to the fact.

Using a dual agent is often compared to getting a divorce and using the same lawyer. If you use the same agent, both the seller and the buyer must question to whom the agent is loyal. Legal or not, this is not a recommended practice.

Q: What if I just happen to fall in love with one of my agent's listings in which he or she represents the seller?

A: Most agents, already committed to representing the seller, will be happy to appoint another agent, generally a coworker, to do all transactions and to act on behalf of you, the buyer. If dual agency is legal in your state, be careful to make known your wish to have someone who represents you in the deal. Some agencies offering duel agency will ask you to sign contracts explaining your legal rights. Make sure you read over the contract very carefully.

Q: Should the whole family go to look at homes?

A: Generally, bringing the whole family along to look at homes is not recommended until you are getting serious about a particular home. While some parents want their children to feel as if they are a part of choosing a new home, think carefully. Are your children up to a grueling day of house hunting? Are you going to be able to give the homes careful consideration if you bring the children along? Does your agent work well with children? If you are planning on taking the children with you, it might be something to discuss with your agent before committing to him or her.

When the question of bringing the children was posed to several agents, most of the agents suggested you leave the children with a sitter until the final selection process and then let them participate in the final decision making.

Q: How many homes should I expect to see in one day?

A: While the availability of your time and the amount of time you take to walk through a property will factor into the number of homes you can expect to see, it is never wise to view more than five or six properties at a time. Even when someone is taking good notes and is focused, after seeing more than six properties, the facts about the homes start to blend together. Staying fresh and alert is important when shopping for a home. If you wear yourself out, you are more likely to miss something, and the process of finding a home could take longer.

Q: What should I take with me to view homes?

A: Because it is easy for you to become so focused on one element of a home that you forget to check out other features, it's always a good idea to have a pen and paper to take notes. Even better than just taking notes, is to make a form with a list of questions to be answered about each home. Some of the questions will be basic information about the home's style, size, and curb appeal, but many of them will depend on what you consider an ideal home. Remember, your real estate agent may have some of the basic information already printed up on sheets for you to take with you. See some sample questions below:

- What style of home is it?
- What was my first impression of its curb appeal?

- Do I like the neighborhood?
- Does it have room in the backyard for me to plant my rose garden?
- Is the master bedroom downstairs and are the closets bigger than the ones in the apartment that are driving me crazy?
- Will I be happy with the counter and cabinet space in the kitchen?
- What are some of the pros of this home? Does this house have something that none of the other homes have had?
- Are there things about this house that I just don't like? Are those things fixable? If the items are fixable, is the house priced so I can afford to make the changes?
- Does the price of this house make it an option?
- On a scale of one to ten, how does this home rate?

While some people want to bring a tape measure to check room sizes and swatches of material to see if the carpet will match their new living room set, it is not recommended that you begin measuring every home or matching color schemes in the beginning process. The time to measure rooms and to see if your sofa will match and fit in the new living room is when you are seriously considering a home. Narrow down your search before you start focusing on the small details.

Q: How many times is too many times to revisit a home?

A: There is no such thing as "too many times." If you are seriously considering a home, you should look at it until you feel certain it is the home that is best for you and your family. Make sure you visit the neighborhood during different times of the day and night. A ride through the area at night may give you some insights you didn't have about the home or neighborhood. Drive to the home during peak travel times to see what the traffic is like. Take a friend or family member you trust with you to see the home, and ask their opinion. It is also recommended that you drive to the neighborhood and walk around. This is a good way to get an honest feel for the area.

If you are still unsure about a property, be honest with your agent about your misgivings or hesitancies about making an offer on the home. He or she may be able to help you look at the situation with a fresh point of view.

Q: Can I take pictures or a video of the home so I can review my findings later?

A: This question is best posed to your agent. With today's digital cameras, many people are opting to use them in their search for the perfect home. It makes sense and is a good way to remember which home had the master suite you liked and which one had the large backyard you loved. However, some agencies are not comfortable with the use of cameras, and even more homeowners are very hesitant about having their homes and belongings photographed. Ultimately, it is wise to remember, you are in someone else's home and should respect their wishes.

Q: What if, after I commit to an agent, I don't feel we are a good match?

A: Buying a home is too important and is too big of an investment to work with someone with whom you're not completely comfortable. However, there are some right ways and wrong ways to end the business relationship. In addition, there can be legal ramifications from walking out of a commitment.

Obviously, if you are not feeling satisfied with the service you're receiving from your agent, you should speak up. If they offer to fix the problem, only you can decide if it is to your benefit to give the agent another chance. If you are in the very beginning of your home shopping search, and the agent hasn't put in long hours assisting you in your search, the agent may be inclined to suggest you find another agent that will better meet your needs.

When questioning the legal ramifications of jumping from one agent to another, the answer depends on several variables. Not only can state regulations and laws influence the answer, but agencies and agents can vary from one to another.

In some cases, even when no contracts have been signed, if an agent has shown you a property and you purchase the same property through another agent, the first agent may be legally entitled to receive a percentage of the commission. If you have signed a buyer's contract, the agent may have legal rights to a commission on any property in the general area that you may purchase.

If you have decided to end the relationship between you and the agent, it is always best to get a signed release from the agent stating you are not liable to pay the agent commission on any property purchase. (This is especially important if you've signed a contract.) Depending on the agent, and perhaps the reason for your request and how much time the agent has spent on your case, he or she may be inclined to give you the release, or they may ask to be compensated for their work. If there is a matter the two of you can't solve, the next step may be to speak with the manager of the agency and then to the state real estate board.

Hopefully, if you sign a contract, you will take the advice given on page 32 and make sure the contract remains in effect for only a short period of time. This reinforces the importance of selecting the right agent and being careful about any contracts you sign.

Q: What should I do if I feel that I'm being excluded from certain neighborhoods?

A: Make your case with the agent to be sure you haven't misinterpreted the situation. Then it is best to contact the U.S. Department of Housing and Urban Development (HUD) if you believe you are being discriminated against on the basis of race, religion, sex, color, nationality, familial status, or disability. The HUD's office of Fair Housing has a hotline to report incidents of discrimination: 1-800-669-9777. For the hearing impaired, you can call: 1-800-927-9275.

Q: What is the difference between a real estate agent and a broker?

A: While real estate agents are state licensed to represent buyers and sellers, brokers have much more stringent licensing requirements. The responsibility of entering into a contract and collecting commissions from the sales of properties falls only to a licensed broker. The real estate offices you visit are owned and generally managed by a broker. The broker oversees all the legal transactions and only through

the licenses of the broker can a real estate deal be brought
to completion.

Q: What is a buyer's broker?

A: In many states, where it is common for an agent to request
a signed agreement with the prospective buyer, this can be a
confusing question. Some people consider any listing agent
with whom you've signed a legal document to be a buyer's
broker, or as some people refer to them, a buyer's agent.

If you do work with an agency that requires buyer contracts, the best piece of advice is to always be aware of what
you're signing. Does it state in the contract who is legally
required to pay for the services of the agent? Does the contract include homes for sale by the owner? What is the length
of time you are committed to work with this agent? (Because
you are committing yourself to this agent, you may want to
limit the contract to as short a time as possible—never more
than two months.) If the agent is working for you, look for
the clauses that explain how any deals are worked if you
happen to choose to purchase a property that is listed by
that same agency. Don't be afraid to ask for amendments to
the contract, and never sign anything that you don't understand or with which you are not comfortable.

A buyer's broker (not just a listing agent who requires
a contract) is an agent who represents only buyers and is
hired by you. The buyer's broker legally acts in the buyer's
best interest, not the seller's. A buyer's broker's goal is to
get the best house for the least amount of money and with
the terms most favorable to you. The commission earned
by the buyer's broker is usually factored into the sale price
of a house and stipulated in the listing agreement. In some

instances, the sellers will even agree to pay full or partial payment to the buyer's broker. However, more and more buyer's brokers work on an hourly basis or for a set fee negotiated in advance. It is advised that you should not pay anything up front for the broker to work for you. Because buyer's brokers may represent only small areas, therefore limiting your home search, signing a contract is not recommended. If you must sign a contract, make it for not more than one or two months.

Q: Do I need a buyer's broker?

A: Some people feel better knowing they have someone working for them and only them. While it is questionable if a buyer's broker can really save you money, if it is peace of mind you're seeking, then it may be worth interviewing one to see if it feels right. Another reason you might consider hiring a buyer's broker is if the market is tight. A buyer's broker's services can be effective when acting for you in homes that are for sale by the owners.

In some states, the concept of buyer's brokers is still relatively new, and many buyers aren't prepared to pay for agency services that they feel they can get for free.

Q: How do I find a buyer's broker?

A: You should have no problem finding a buyer's broker in any major metropolitan area. Ask your local realty board, consult the telephone directory, or contact any of the leading buyer's broker organizations who will make referrals to their members. These include the Home Referral Network

(1-800-500-3569, *www.finderhome.com*) and the National Association of Exclusive Buyer Agents (*www.naeba.org*).

Q: Do I need a lawyer to purchase a home?

A: The answer to this question will vary depending on the state you are living in. Some states require a lawyer to assist in several areas of the homebuying process whereas other states make no such provisions as long as a qualified real estate professional is involved in the deal.

Even when a state doesn't require a lawyer, some people opt to hire one to help with the complex paperwork and legal contracts. A lawyer can review contracts, make you aware of special considerations, and assist you with the closing process. To find a lawyer who is experienced in representing homebuyers, ask your real estate agent to recommend one. If your agent doesn't have any names, shop around by using the Yellow Pages or asking friends and/or family about their attorneys. Make sure you get a detailed list of what services the lawyer is providing and the cost of his or her fees so no unexpected surprises await you. Hiring an attorney should alleviate some of the stress of the homebuying procedure, not add to it.

Q: What does it mean to be preapproved?

A: Being preapproved means you apply for a mortgage as if you have already found the house and are ready to purchase the property. The lender reviews your qualifications; checks your credit report, your debt, and your income; and either approves or rejects the loan. He will provide you with a letter or certificate stating that the lender will actually fund the loan, pending an appraisal of the property, title report, and purchase contract.

Q: What is the difference between being preapproved and being prequalified?

A: Being prequalified means you have spoken with someone about the possibility of acquiring a loan, and after calculating your income and average debt, they have run some figures to see approximately how much the lender might agree to loan. The key word is might, for until the lender has checked your credit report and gotten documentation on your income and debt, it will not make any agreements. Basically, you walk away with no guarantee of a loan.

Q: Should I be preapproved for a home loan?

A: Yes. We've all heard of someone with a beer budget and champagne taste. There is nothing wrong with fine taste or wanting the most home for your money, but knowing what you can afford will save you and your agent a lot of time and frustration.

While the approval process requires some personal questions about your finances and therefore can be uncomfortable, it is considered almost essential in most markets. While some agents require you to be preapproved and others will take you on after only being prequalified, being preapproved can greatly affect the outcome of your home search.

First, an agent is more likely to take you seriously if you show him or her that you're serious about purchasing a home and not just someone interested in checking out floor plans or getting decorating tips. One way to show the agent your true intentions is to have the loan secure.

In some cases, an agent can use your preapproval as a bargaining chip when talking about price. The agent may tell the seller, "My clients are ready to buy; they have the loan secured only for this amount." The seller, knowing they have a sure deal on the table, may be more inclined to negotiate.

Another example where the preapproval can be advantageous is in a tight market. If two offers come in for a home at the same time, one with and one without approval, generally speaking, the buyer with the approval will win the bid. Basically, the sellers are going to say, "Show me the money," and the first one to comply gets the property.

Q: Does it cost anything to be preapproved?

A: While each lender may vary, generally, the homebuyer will have to pay for only the cost of a credit report fee. (However, some companies do require application fees.) In most cases, credit report fees run approximately $60 to $75. (More information about loan fees and the preapproval process can be found in the "Loan Wisdom" section.)

Q: If I'm just getting preapproved to start looking for a home, do I really need to be selective of which lender I choose to do the preapproval process?

A: While some people want to get preapproved only so they can get started shopping for a home, it is wise to slow down and think about the consequences.

The first thing to consider is that each time your credit is reviewed, your overall credit score could drop. One should also think about the cost of being preapproved. If you are paying application fees, are you prepared to pay them again later? One should also consider the time it will take to shop for the loan after you've found the perfect house. If it is a tight market, and the seller has more than one offer, you may be compelled to go with the preapproval lender without having the opportunity to shop for the best loan. (See the section "Loan Wisdom" for questions about shopping for a loan.)

Q: Is my credit good enough to buy a home?

A: Do you have some outstanding debt? Have you paid your bills on time? Do you even have credit? Some people might know how they will stand up to a credit report; however, many first-time buyers are unsure. Even those who are experienced with the credit process might not be sure how their credit rates.

Exposing your credit records can be, for some, the most difficult part of the homebuying process. However, homebuyers should know that very few people have perfect credit histories. Think of your credit report as sort of a test grade. We would all like to ace the test, but making a high B is not too bad. And when you take into consideration some outside, life-altering circumstance such as a divorce or the death of a loved one, maintaining even a C average can be acceptable. You don't have to have a "perfect" credit report to get approved for a loan. This isn't to say that you can't and won't be turned down for a loan if you have some serious black marks against you. It is also wise to know that the quality of your loan, interest rates, and such can be affected by your credit history. But you should not let the fear of having your credit checked stop you from proceeding with your goal of buying a home.

The best thing you can do is get a copy of your credit report now so you can see where you stand before you apply for a loan. It is advised that you review your credit report weeks, even months, prior to applying for a loan. That way, if there are mistakes on your report, you can correct them before it is viewed by the lender. If you realize how little credit you have, you might start looking for ways to build your credit before you apply for a loan.

Q: How can I check my credit, and do I have to pay for it?

A: You can get a copy of your credit report by contacting any of the three following national bureaus:

> *Equifax*
> P.O. Box 740241
> Atlanta, GA 30348
> Phone: (888) 685-1111
> Online: *www.equifax.com*
>
> *Experian*
> P.O. Box 2104
> Allen, TX 75013
> Phone: (888) 397-3742
> Online: *www.experian.com*

Trans Union
P.O. Box 1000
Chester, PA 19022
Phone: (800) 888-4213
Online: *www.transunion.com*

By law, you have the right to obtain a copy of your own credit report at a reasonable price. Typically, the fee for a copy of your report will run about $9. However, in the states of Colorado, Georgia, Maryland, Massachusetts, New Jersey, and Vermont, residents are entitled to get free copies periodically.

You may also be eligible to receive a discounted or free credit report if you meet one of the following conditions:

- Your request for credit was denied. (Some of the bureaus may offer a free copy only after a specified amount of time, such as sixty days.)
- Adverse action, such as an interest rate increase, was taken against you based on information on your credit report. (The name of the credit bureau that provided your credit report and how to contact them for a copy should be provided by the company that declined your credit application or took adverse action.)
- If you certify in writing that you are unemployed and seeking employment or receive public welfare assistance.
- If you have reason to believe your credit file contains inaccuracies resulting from fraud.

To confirm your eligibility and request a free copy, contact one of the bureaus.

Q: What is a credit bureau?

A: A credit reporting agency or bureau is a business that gathers, maintains, and sells information about consumer's credit histories. The agencies collect information about consumers' payment habits from credit grantors like banks, credit unions, savings and loans, finance companies, and retailers. The information is stored in computer databases, and the company sells the information to other credit grantors in the form of credit reports.

When anyone applies for a new credit card or loan, the lender orders your credit report from at least one credit bureau. There are three major credit bureaus that provide nationwide coverage of consumer credit information in the United States.

Q: If there are three major credit bureaus, will all three reports be the same?

A: Not necessarily. While most national lending institutions report consumer credit information to all three bureaus, smaller banks or small credit grantors may report to only one—and in some cases, small credit grantors may not report to any. Therefore, a credit report from one bureau may differ from a report from another.

Q: What is a credit report and what information does a credit report include?

A: A credit report is a document that reports your credit payment history, the level of debt you have, and how many credit cards and loans you have. Most of the companies from which you've borrowed money—credit card companies, department stores, banks, student loan associations—will make reports of your payment habits every two or three years to one or all of the three major credit bureaus. These habits may include: late payments, missed payments, and, hopefully, on-time payments.

Your credit report contains:

- Your name, current and previous addresses, phone number, Social Security number, date of birth, and current and previous employers.
- Federal district bankruptcy records and state and county court records of tax liens and monetary judgments.
- Particular data about each account, such as credit limit or loan amount, date the account was opened, balance, monthly payment, and payment habits during the past several years.
- The names of everyone who has obtained a copy of your credit report.
- Statements of dispute, which allow both creditors and consumers to report the factual history of an account.

Q: What are the red flags that may prevent me from getting a loan?

A: While one and even more of these items may not keep you from getting a loan, these are things lenders don't want to see: late payments, recent credit inquires (however, they have altered how they view these, and they are no longer as big of a problem as they used to be), overextended credit, paycheck garnishments, bankruptcy, and liens.

Q: What if it isn't bad credit holding me back, but rather no credit?

A: While it seems to be an ideal to be debt-free and never owe anyone, the truth is that establishing credit is important. While no credit isn't bad credit, the fact is that just as bad credit can keep you from getting a home loan, not having established credit can also be a deterrent when you apply for a mortgage. In most cases, a lack of credit doesn't necessarily mean you will be turned down, but chances are you will be seen as a risky borrower and may not be able to apply for the primo loans with the best options. There are various options, however, and you should discuss this with the lender. (For more information on loans, and those more willing to work with riskier homebuyers, see the "Loan Wisdom" section.)

Those people who are concerned about the no-credit issue might be surprised at what some lenders see as alternative credit. Cell phone bills, utilities bills, even monthly rent—if paid regularly and on time—can be considered as alternative credit.

Q: How can I start building my credit?

A: Start small and build it up slowly. Get a credit card that has a small credit limit, maybe one from a local department store or a financial institution. Remember, even one late payment may put a less-than-shining mark on your credit, so be sure you are prepared to deal with making timely payments. After six months, apply for another card and continue paying the monthly payments in a timely manner.

It is good to note that where credit is concerned, quantity doesn't outweigh quality. Two or three small credit cards will not be viewed as favorably as a car loan. So as soon as you have established the smaller credit, go for the bigger item that will really give your credit some merit.

Q: How long does it take to build one's credit?

A: Generally, a lender will want to see a year to two years of credit history. Remember, the less credit you have, the more important it is that you show good credit history. Avoiding late payments and any other black marks is very important to one trying to get approved for a loan with a shorter credit history.

Q: Does a credit bureau approve or deny credit?

A: No. The credit bureaus do not grant or deny your loan. In the case of bad credit, it is easy to want to shoot the messenger, but homebuyers need to know that the bureaus do not make the decisions. It is up to individual lenders to evaluate your credit report and any other factors they consider important and then decide whether or not they approve the loan.

The bureaus do, however, give you a score. Lenders use these scores to help evaluate your credit. Yet each lender has their different methods of viewing scores and different ways of figuring them into your loan approval.

Q: What is a credit risk score?

A: This magical, mysterious number means a lot. Your credit score, also known as your FICO (named after Fair, Isaac and Company) score, is a statistical analysis of the likelihood that you will repay the loan on time. The way a bureau figures your score is a complicated process that draws from approximately 100 variables in your credit report. Included in these variables are delinquent bills, outstanding debts, the number and amount of balances you owe, and your credit history in general.

Your credit score is not affected by your race, religious preference, medical history, lifestyle, personal background, political preference, or even your criminal record.

Your credit score is a number between 400 and 900. Most lenders consider the magic number to be anything over 620. If you score anything above a 680, you will likely be considered a premium borrower. If your score is below a 620, your loan may be declined.

One reason this number is so mysterious is that most borrowers never see their scores. Because the numbers are viewed differently from lender to lender, your copy from the bureaus will not include the score. However, you may request a copy of your report from the lender, which should have this information included.

Q: How can a high credit score help me?

A: Not only will a high score get you approved for a loan, but it can also make you eligible for lower interest rates and better terms. In addition, a high score may speed up the loan process overall because there may be no need to have someone review the data received from the bureau. Some lenders are automating at least part of the home loan business, doing less evaluating and giving people with higher scores automatic acceptance. While this is good for those with good credit ratings, those who have borderline scores may find it to their disadvantage.

Q: How long does information stay on my credit report?

A: The good news is that "active" positive information can have a longer life expectancy than negative information. To be considered active, information has to be forthcoming on an account. Yet the data is not considered inactive for seven years. This means that, if you are paying a loan on time, even a thirty-year loan, this information may stay on your report for the life of a loan and for another seven years after the loan has been closed. Thus, a closed account will disappear from your report seven years after it is reported as closed.

Most negative information, such as missed payments and public record items, remains on a report for only up to seven years—even if the account is still active. Bankruptcies generally will remain on your report for ten years, and unpaid tax liens will remain for fifteen years. Most inquiries stay on your report up to two years.

Q: What is a mortgage report?

A: A mortgage report is a compilation of data gathered by a mortgage company and used to evaluate you as a borrower. The mortgage report is compiled from credit reports from two or three credit bureaus. The lender purchases the credit reports, combines them, and manually evaluates specific information such as employment, balances of credit accounts, and public record information such as any liens and bankruptcies.

Q: Who may check my credit report?

A: Federal law regulates who can attain a copy of your credit report and for what purpose the information can be used. Before a business can apply for a copy of your credit report, they must meet the following requirements:

- Proof of a permissible purpose under federal law
- A background check of the on-site inspection of the business
- A current business license
- A signed contract requiring the business to use the data properly

Q: What if I find something on my credit that is false?

A: If you come across some information that is wrong, first contact the source of the information and ask them to clear up the mistake. Immediately afterward, it is advised to contact the credit bureau of the mistake. Federal law allows consumers to challenge inaccuracies and correct their credit files.

The bureau should provide you with a form for you to make the claim of an inaccuracy. After you have submitted the form, the bureau has thirty days to investigate the complaint.

If you are correct, or if the creditor who gave you the bad mark can no longer verify the information, the credit bureau must remove those marks from your report. If, for whatever reason, the bureau agrees with the creditor, you will be given the results from their investigation.

Q: If I'm turned down due to my credit by one lender, will I be turned down by all?

A: Not necessarily. As stated earlier, each lender has a different way of viewing credit reports and reacting to credit scores. When you have credit that is questionable, it may mean you will have to shop around more and you may have to look at alternate loan types, which may lead to higher down payments or higher interest rates. (See the "Loan Wisdom" section for information on what options may be open to you if you have a less-than-shining credit report.)

Q: My lender said I have an A rating; what is this rating and what does it mean?

A: After compiling a mortgage report, lenders generally rate borrowers from A to E. (An A rating is given to borrowers who have the strongest potential for repaying the loan in a timely manner.) If you have too many negative marks against your credit, you may be given a C rating. As a C-rated borrower, you may be expected to pay a higher down payment (20 to 35 percent of the price of the home) and the interest rate may jump one to three points higher than that of an A-rated borrower.

In some cases, if your credit rating is lower than an A, you might have to bypass commercial banks and find a mortgage broker that specializes in difficult loans.

Q: What if I've had credit in the past and paid my bills on time, but it's not showing up on my report?

A: While most lenders do report to at least one of the major credit bureaus, the truth is that they are not required by law to do so. The Fair Credit Reporting Act only specifies what must be done if a lender chooses to report information or review your credit history.

In most instances, the only lenders who do not report to bureaus are the smaller lenders who have not subscribed to a credit bureau—having subscribed means the lender has filled out the required paperwork and agrees to the conditions of the bureau. While you cannot force a lender to comply, you can ask them to report your account information. If they are a subscriber, they may report the information if asked. If they are not, they may decline. For this reason, anyone who is working on establishing credit, or anyone attempting to rebuild positive credit, should always ask potential lenders if they subscribe to credit bureaus.

Q: What are some quick steps I can take to improve how my credit appears in the near future?

A: First, get a copy of your credit report. Read over it carefully to make sure there aren't any mistakes. If you find errors, start correcting those immediately. (See pages 46–47 for information on correcting false information.) Then check all bad marks and make sure they are not outdated. (See page 45 for information on how long information stays on a credit report.) If things have passed the determined amount of time that they should appear, contact the credit bureau and ask for these items to be removed. After you have dealt with inaccuracies and cleaned up what no longer should be reported, start working on things that are the easiest to change.

Are there any black marks that you can take care of now? Perhaps you neglected to pay for a book from a mail-order book club you belonged to several years back or there is a department store bill that fell through the cracks. Even a small unpaid bill of less than $100 could be a deterrent to your getting a home loan. When you pay off delinquent bills, make sure you get something in writing from the company that states that you have taken care of the problem. Then make copies of the letter and your canceled check and send these to the credit bureau.

If you have any liens on your credit report, these will need to be cleared up immediately. Getting a home loan with a lien on your credit report is almost impossible.

Now look at all the accounts, like credit cards, you applied for but haven't used in years. Too many open accounts lowers your credit score, so you would be wise to close accounts that are not active. Make sure that these accounts, and others that have been recently closed, are labeled "closed by consumer" in the report.

One of the main objectives of checking your credit is to see how much you owe, so the lender can then figure out how much you can realistically afford. It is wise to pay off as many bills as possible, to reduce your debt load, before applying for a loan. However, chances are the money in your savings has been set aside for the down payment. The pros and cons of paying off debt versus having a larger down payment depend on numerous circumstances, including how much money you really owe, your credit history in general, how much money you'll be borrowing, and the type of loan for which you'll be applying. The right option for you may depend on whether one or the other will prevent you from getting the loan. If you cannot receive approval with the amount of debt you have, the only option you might have is to pay off the debt and check into loans with lower down-payment possibilities. On the flip side, you might be able to squeak by with your current amount of debt and get the loan if you have a substantial down payment.

If you find yourself in this tight of a situation, you may want to talk to a financial advisor or to a broker you trust to give you the best advice. A professional should be able to show you the long-term effects of each option. If your situation is really tight, however, don't be surprised if they suggest you postpone buying until you have alleviated at least some of your financial responsibilities. (See pages 8–10 for more information on where to look for the cash for a down payment.)

The last piece of advice for cleaning up your credit report is to look at any other black marks and ask yourself if there is a good explanation. Were you late paying bills last year because you were laid off or because you had a serious surgery or illness? Was there a divorce or perhaps a death in the family? If there is an understandable reason for those black marks, write a letter to the credit bureau and ask them to affix it to your report to serve as an explanation to any lenders.

Q: I have good credit but very little money for a down payment—can I buy a house?

A: Yes. There are home loans and government programs that offer options and help with down payments. (See the "Loan Wisdom" section for information about low down-payment options.)

Q: How do I start to repair bad credit?

A: The good news is that you can pick up the pieces and start building a positive credit report because your credit profile is always evolving. The first step is to look at how you can begin to meet your past lender's needs. Can you work out an arrangement to play catch-up? Can you pay off any of the delinquent accounts? Bankruptcy should be considered only as a last resort.

Help is available if you're having a difficult time paying bills. The nonprofit National Foundation of Credit Counseling (NFCC) (1-800-388-2227) will assist you in establishing a budget that will facilitate repaying your creditors. Other organizations offer quality credit counseling as well. However, you should be sure that the organization is nonprofit and provides budgeting and financial management training in addition to any debt-management plan, and does so at little or no cost. Be leery of any organization/company that claims it can provide a quick fix to your credit problems, that does not provide you with financial management education, or that charges substantial fees for its service.

When it comes down to establishing new credit, it is much like starting out to build your credit—start small and build up slowly. Go for small accounts, or take out small loans on inexpensive items and pay them off promptly. Because of your past record, you may have to pay higher interest rates. Be forewarned that from here on out, your bill-paying pattern is critical. Your behavior during the next eighteen to twenty-four months will be scrutinized by any future lender.

Q: How long does it take to repair bad credit?

A: The answer to this question depends on how bad your credit is. While late payments and such can stay on your record for seven years and will alert any lender of past problems, a period of eighteen to twenty-four months of good paying patterns may offset a few negative checks.

If the negative marks were more severe, bills that were never paid, liens, and even bankruptcy, the answer to how long it might take to repair the damage may come from seeing how, or if, those situations were reconciled. If the accounts are now being met, or have been marked paid, a lender may again look to the last eighteen to twenty-four months of credit history to make its decision.

Another factor figured into the time it may take to repair the damage from past credit sins, is the circumstances surrounding the events. If you have written a letter explaining your problems, such as being laid off, and have had it attached to your files, a lender may be quicker to overlook past mistakes.

Q: I applied for bankruptcy in the past; can I get a home loan?

A: While bankruptcy is definitely a red flag, one that is more serious than late payments, this isn't to say that you won't be approved for a home loan. Preparing yourself to face the obvious hurdles, and knowing what you are likely to be up against, is the best way to approach this problem. Below is a list of things you might anticipate, and be prepared for, if shopping for a loan under these circumstances:

- Be prepared for a good deal of shopping around among lenders.
- Be ready to field questions about what caused the bankruptcy. Be prepared to tell the truth about your situation. It is wise to appear remorseful and apologetic, not casual or cavalier.
- You might have to go to a mortgage broker who knows lenders who deal with high-risk borrowers.
- You will probably have to accept alternative loans with higher interest rates.
- Expect to have to pay a higher down payment than the normal 10 to 15 percent.
- Know that you will need to have a scrupulously clean credit report since the bankruptcy.
- Be prepared to wait awhile after you applied for bankruptcy before applying for a loan. While, legally, there are no time limits on how soon you can secure a conventional mortgage after a bankruptcy is discharged, it is unlikely that a lender will take a chance on you until it can see you've made some changes in your financial situation. This isn't to say that there aren't some conventional lenders who will turn you down no matter how long ago the bankruptcy

occurred, but most lenders believe in second chances. With Federal Housing Administration (FHA)–insured loans, a bankruptcy must be discharged for at least one year; the Department of Veterans Affairs insists on a two-year wait with VA loans.

Q: Are there options for me if I really want to buy a house right now but my credit isn't any good?

A: There's a fair chance that even with bad credit you can secure a loan. However, you will have to consider some less conventional methods of securing a mortgage. These methods are not as common as a "standard" loan from a bank. They will probably come with a higher cost in the long run, higher interest rates, and higher points, but they may be less stringent about qualifications. (For more detailed information on home loans, see the "Loan Wisdom" section.)

Part Two

Loan Wisdom

For most people, acquiring a loan is by far the most dreaded part of the homebuying experience. Perhaps what we fear is sitting across from a stiff-shouldered lender who is scrutinizing our credit report with an unreadable expression, or maybe it's all the loan jargon they use, which sounds like a foreign language and makes our heads swim. It's true, we all get a little edgy at the idea of someone sifting through our personal data. And while nothing can change the fact that the lender will review your credit, hopefully the information covered in this section will make this step a little easier and make the jargon a lot less confusing.

It is in this section that you will find questions and answers that will help you decide on the best loan plan for your situation. It covers everything from conventional loans to FHA options. You'll learn why fixed-rate loans are the best choice for some people, while others come out ahead by going with an adjustable rate mortgage (ARM) rate. You'll discover the right questions to ask the lender, how to differentiate one mortgage company from another, and what type of loans offer lower down-payment options.

The goal of this section is to make you an informed consumer, to prepare you, not just to get a loan, but to get the right loan, one that can save you hundreds, sometimes thousands, of dollars over the life of your loan.

Q: What is a mortgage?

A: Using generalities, a mortgage is a loan obtained to purchase real estate. The mortgage itself is a lien (a legal claim) on the home or property that secures the promise to pay the debt. All mortgages have two features: principal and interest.

Principal is best defined as either the amount of money borrowed or the amount of money still owed. Interest is the fee paid for the use of money.

Q: What is leveraging and why is it important?

A: Leveraging is the effective use of money to buy property by using the smallest amount of one's own capital and borrowing as much as possible in order to obtain the maximum percentage of return on the original investment. When considering leverage, you look at how much the home is expected to appreciate and measure it against how and when it would be financially in your favor to sell the property.

While all homeowners want their home to be a solid investment, leveraging is a bigger concern for those who are looking to sell their properties in the near future. If you are buying your first home and hope to get a bigger home or one in a more established neighborhood in the near future, you should ask your real estate agent about the homes that may offer the better leverage and attempt to get a loan that will require the lowest amount of investment from you.

Q: What factors determine the amount of my monthly mortgage payment?

A: There are numerous factors that will be considered to determine the amount of your monthly payment. The amount of the down payment, the size of the mortgage, the interest rate, the length of the loan's term, and the payment schedule will all come into play in setting a dollar amount on the payments.

Q: What is included in a monthly mortgage payment?

A: For the most part, the monthly mortgage payment mainly pays off the principal and interest. However, many lenders also include local real estate taxes, homeowner's insurance, and mortgage insurance (when applicable).

Q: What is equity?

A: Equity is the amount of a home that you own outright, not including the mortgage or any other debts against it.

Q: What is a loan to value (LTV) ratio and how does it determine the size of my loan?

A: The LTV ratio is the amount of loan money compared with the price or the appraised value of the property you are buying. Every loan has a specific LTV limit. For example, if you had a 95 percent LTV loan on a home priced at $50,000, you could borrow up to 95 percent of the $50,000 ($47,500) and would have to pay the remaining amount of $2,500 as a down payment.

The LTV ratio reflects the amount of equity borrowers have in their homes. A high LTV means the homebuyers are required to pay less out of their own funds. For this reason, lenders wanting to protect themselves against potential loss in case of default will usually require mortgage insurance on loans with LTVs of 80 percent or more.

Q: What are points?

A: Many times referred to as discount points, points are essentially prepaid interest. Each point equals 1 percent of the total loan amount. Discount points allow you to lower your interest rate.

Generally, for each point paid on a thirty-year mortgage, the interest rate is lowered by one-eighth (or 0.125) of a percentage point. To see what point percentage works best for you, ask your lender for an interest rate with zero points and compare how much your rate decreases with each point paid.

Discount points are usually considered good if you plan to stay in a home for some time, because they can lower the monthly loan payment. Points are also tax deductible when you purchase a home, and you may be able to negotiate for the seller to pay for some of them.

Q: Why is it so important to shop for a lender? Aren't all lenders the same?

A: All lenders are not created equal, so finding the best lender is very important. Everything from types of loans, interest rates, and fees can vary from one lender to the next. You can even be turned down by one lender and accepted by another using the same credit report.

Just as you should not buy the first house you see without shopping around, you should not go with the first lender without doing your homework.

Q: When is really the right time to shop for a loan?

A: There was a time when you didn't shop for a loan until you had found the house you wanted. Times have changed. As advised earlier, you really need to shop for a loan before you shop for houses. Being preapproved for a loan will make house hunting a lot easier.

Q: How do I start to shop for lenders?

A: Many entities, including credit unions, banks, savings and loans, insurance companies, and mortgage bankers, make home loans. Lenders and terms are constantly changing as new companies appear, old ones merge, and market conditions fluctuate. To find the best lender, you should compare loans and their fees with at least six lenders. While this may be time consuming, the process can save you thousands of dollars.

You can also start loan shopping by asking for recommendations. However, be aware that the advice could be tainted. For example, if your real estate agent recommends his or her favorite lender, it may not mean they can offer you the best deal. In fact, there's a chance the lender paid your broker a fee for the referral—a practice that is illegal but often found.

Q: What do I look for in a lender?

A: Besides the loan that offers you the best financial advantages, a good lender must be financially stable and have a reputation for customer satisfaction. Be sure to choose a company that offers helpful advice and makes you feel comfortable enough to ask questions and request explanations of the things you don't quite understand. There are too many important factors about your loan for you not to completely understand the process.

It is also recommended you find a lender who has the authority to approve and process your loan locally, since it will be easier for you to monitor the status of your application and ask questions. A local lender is also encouraged because they know the home values and conditions in your state.

Q: What should I bring with me when I apply for a loan?

A: It can't be helped, there's a lot of paperwork involved in applying for a loan. However, by being prepared and having the needed documents and files, you'll save yourself a lot of frustration. Below is a list of necessary materials you will want to bring with you when you apply for a loan:

- Recent address(es): Make a list of all the places you have lived in the past two years.
- List of assets: Assets include holdings such as stocks and bonds (if you have an account with a stock brokerage firm, make sure to bring a recent statement), IRA account(s), vested retirement plans, surrender value of life insurance policies, cars, and any other property such

as RVs. Don't forget to include current balances, names and addresses of institutions, and the account numbers when applicable.

- List of debts: You should include credit cards, auto loans, school loans, and any other money owed. Include the addresses, account numbers, balances, and monthly payment requirements.
- Divorce papers and child support agreements: If you receive child support, you may choose to have this income considered to help you secure the mortgage.
- Paperwork for any extra income: This has to be a regular source of income, such as a second job or perhaps rental payments from a family member.
- Foreclosure and bankruptcy status: This information should be given up-front because the lender will probably find out anyway, and any attempt on your part to hide the information will be viewed unfavorably.
- Gift letter: If someone is helping you with the down payment, you will need a letter stating that the money is a gift and is not expected to be repaid.
- Income and employment records: You will need to collect W-2 statements for the last two years and pay stubs from the previous month. If you are self-employed, bring your federal tax returns for the last two years.
- Social Security number: Instead of having just your Social Security number, it is a good idea to bring your card with you.
- VA documentation: If you are applying for a VA-backed loan, you need a Certificate of Eligibility. Some lenders have access to the automated Certificate of Eligibility (ACE); however, not all cases can be processed this way, and sometimes VA documentation can take up to eight weeks to arrive.

Q: Can I get information on mortgages online?

A: Yes. There are two basic types of mortgage sites: those that offer loans and those that do not (no-loan sites). Both types can be valuable tools in your search for a lender and a loan.

A growing number of today's computer-savvy consumers are browsing the Web to find the perfect mortgage. You can even complete an online mortgage application while sitting in front of your computer. However, most consumers, even people who don't mind purchasing hundreds of dollars of merchandise on the Internet, still find it scary to complete their mortgage transaction without the benefit of a "live" mortgage broker or lender. This isn't to say that you shouldn't check out the sources yourself. The twenty-four-hour convenience of exploring your options is no doubt a benefit.

Q: What can I learn on a no-loan site, and what are the Web addresses?

A: No-loan sites have a wealth of mortgage information. There are vast libraries of mortgage information on the Web that can help you understand the loan process and the lingo. These sites are great places to examine mortgage programs, understand loan qualifications, use online mortgage calculators, and check your credit. Look at such sites as *www.HSH. com* and *www.bankrate.com* for daily tabs on mortgage rates, indexes, and market events that push cost up and down. You will also be able to attain the latest regional average rates on purchase, refinance, equity, and other mortgages. The no-loan sites are often called referral sites because they introduce you to a host of participating lenders. You will find the lenders information through either links or advertisements.

While surfing the net for mortgage information, don't neglect to check out the informative government, quasi-government, and trade sites such as Fannie Mae (*www.fanniemae.com*), the U.S. Department of Housing and Urban Development (*www.hud.gov*), Freddie Mac (*www.freddiemac.com*), and the Mortgage Bankers Association (*www.mbaa.org*). As your fingers brush over the keyboard, you'll find information about the latest mortgage programs and conforming loan amount changes. They also provide complaint services for mortgage problems on and off the Net.

Q: Can I really get approved for a loan on the Internet?

A: Yes. Online mortgage sites do offer direct access to loans. However, securing loans online isn't for everyone. Window shopping for online mortgages is a lot easier than actually completing the application process electronically. It is wise to remember that, if something goes wrong, you can't just sit down face-to-face with your computer and work it out.

Q: Are all online mortgage sites the same?

A: No. Just as lenders vary from one to another, so do online mortgage sites. There are three varieties of mortgage sites that offer loans. Below are descriptions of each:

Single or Direct Lender Sites
Most mortgage Web sites are direct lender sites. These include mortgage lenders such as Countrywide (*www.countrywide.com*) as well as banks that offer mortgage loans, such as Bank of America (*www.bankofamerica.com*) and

Wells Fargo (*www.wellsfargo.com*). In addition to applying for a loan online, you may want to visit a lender's site to further investigate their programs. To find a particular lender, search for the name of the financial institution on the Internet. You should know that these sites rarely provide complete product price information (points, fees, and such), but you can find basic facts that may help you with your decision.

Auction Sites

These sites allow you to complete a loan application, which is forwarded to lenders who, in turn, will compete for your business. Because some of the lenders are subprime, consumers with less than shining credit may find options here. Be aware that it may take a few days to get several offers. If you want to compare more loans, you can repeat the process on different sites, for not all sites are viewed by the same lenders. Auction sites include *www.lendingtree.com* and *www.RealEstate.com*.

Multilender Sites

Here you will not be required to fill out an application before you shop for mortgages. This is a good way to really see how the variables of a loan, APRs (meaning "annual percentage rate"), points, and such will play out in your particular case. You enter your loan amount, property details, and other needed information, and you'll get lenders coming back with their best rates, APRs, points, even settlement costs. If you then choose to fill out an application, the site will review and process your application and send it to a possible lender. It's worth mentioning that many consumers have complained of the service they received when they dealt with multilender sites.

Q: What should I know before completing an online mortgage?

A: There are several things you should be aware of and consider before you decide to apply online.

- Be educated about the mortgage process. Know what you are doing; don't let the ease of doing this via the computer stop you from doing your homework.
- Double-check to make sure the online broker is licensed and regulated by your state.
- Don't forget to check out the lender. To verify the lender's status with the Federal Deposit Insurance Corp., go to *www.fdic.gov*.
- Don't forget that each time you fill out an application, your credit will be checked, and too many credit checks can affect your credit score.
- Get a rate lock. Whether you are applying online or off, ask for your rate to be guaranteed, in case interest rates rise. Make sure you get this guarantee in writing.
- Consider the security issues of giving your personal information online. While the chance is low that someone could steal the information, it is always best to be aware of the possibility.
- If something reads too good to be true, know that it probably is. The average consumer has gotten better at knowing a line when he or she hears it, but often reading something on a dedicated online site gives us a false sense of security. Don't be fooled.

Q: What is the best way to compare loan terms between lenders, both online and off?

A: The best way to compare loan terms is to devise a checklist for the information from each lender. This checklist should contain:

- The company's name and basic information such as address and phone number
- The type of mortgages it offers
- The minimum down payment it requires
- Interest rate and points
- Closing costs
- If they charge the origination fees at the time of preapproval
- Loan process time
- Prepayment penalties
- Notes of the rapport you find with the mortgage broker and the overall feeling that he or she will help you find the best deal

While shopping for a loan can be done on the phone, in person, or on the Internet, a face-to-face interview is recommended before making a final decision. Also keep in mind that you must speak with lenders on the same day, because interest rates can go up or down overnight.

Q: I've been preapproved by a lender; is it too late to shop for the best loan now?

A: No, it is not too late. The right loan could save you thousands of dollars. However, it would have been wise to have shopped before you were preapproved, because now you may have to pay another credit-reporting fee. Also, application fees (if you paid one to the preapproval lender) are generally nonrefundable.

You need to keep in mind that having your credit checked can affect your credit score. Another thing that may factor into the wisdom of changing lenders is if you had the interest rate locked in at the time of preapproval. If so, and interest rates have since risen, you need to make sure you compare those rates to the "better deal" you may be receiving with a new lender.

Q: How long does it take to be preapproved for a loan?

A: This question varies widely from lender to lender. While most companies take one to six weeks to really confirm an approval, there are some who can review your credit, confirm income, and give you an answer in less than an hour. Be aware, however, that they will probably continue to do their evaluation and if they discover something not previously known, it could affect the outcome of your loan.

Q: What is RESPA?

A: RESPA stands for Real Estate Settlement Procedures Act. It mandates lenders to disclose information to potential customers throughout the mortgage process. Thus, it protects borrowers from abuses by lending institutions. RESPA requires that lenders fully inform borrowers about all closing costs, lend servicing and escrow account practices, and business relationships between closing service providers and other parties involved in the transaction.

For more information on RESPA, call 1-800-569-4287 for a local counseling referral. Or check out *www.hud.gov.*

Q: Where can I get a copy of the RESPA?

A: Your real estate agent may give you a copy of the RESPA booklet after your offer for a home has been accepted, or it may come from the lender with your loan package. If you don't receive one, ask for a copy.

Q: What is a good-faith estimate?

A: A good-faith estimate is an approximation of all fees to be paid by you before closing. It includes all closing costs and any escrow costs you will encounter when purchasing a home. The lender must supply it within three days of your application so that you can make accurate judgments in your search for the best loan.

Q: How can I protect myself against loan fraud?

A: With today's numerous organizations and regulations like RESPA, consumers are more protected now than in the past, but it is still wise to be careful. To ensure you don't fall victim to loan fraud, and to protect yourself from any legal allegations from the lender, follow these steps as you apply for a loan:

- Make certain you read and understand everything you sign.

- Do not sign any blank documents under any circumstances.
- Do not purchase property for someone else.
- Be honest about the length of time you have been employed.
- Do not exaggerate your income or assets.
- Make certain you report all your debts.
- Do not alter your income tax returns for any reason.
- Tell the truth about gifts and financial help you've acquired to make the down payment.
- Be truthful about your credit problems.
- Do not mislead anyone on your intention of occupying the home.
- Do not provide any false documentation.

Q: What is an amortization table?

A: An amortization table is a chart that shows the amount of principal and interest due at regular intervals. It is a great tool to compare interest rates and loan payments. For example, with an amortization table, you will be able to compare monthly payment amounts of a fifteen-year loan to those of a thirty-year loan. You can also use it to compare differences in monthly payments with different rates. Most lenders will provide you with an amortization table if you request it.

Q: Exactly what is APR?

A: As stated earlier, APR stands for "annual percentage rate." This term is often used in advertisements for loans.

An APR is an average interest rate that combines the projected payments on the loan plus certain up-front loan costs (such as points, origination fees, and other costs of obtaining the loan) over a certain period of time. It was designed by the federal government to give homebuyers a uniform measure of the cost of credit to compare mortgages.

Q: Will the best APR be the lowest?

A: Generally speaking, the lower the APR, the better the monetary savings. However, as with lower interest rates, the benefits of a low APR are better designated for consumers who plan to hold the loan for its entire term. The lower the APR, the more likely you are to see larger up-front fees.

To adequately compare APRs, you need a modified APR chart. This chart factors in the length of time you plan to hold the loan to give you an idea of the savings and overall costs. If an APR chart is not available, ask your lender to do the numbers.

Q: So, should I shop for a loan comparing APRs, or should I be comparing interest rates?

A: Shopping for a home can be confusing. Add all the variables into the picture and it can become overwhelming. But relax, here's a good rule of thumb that will help you decide if you should be looking at APRs or interest rates. If you're going to keep your home more than ten years, go ahead and use APRs to compare loans. If not, shop for interest rates and ask your lender for a list of loan costs for each loan you consider, so you can compare.

Q: Exactly how does the interest rate factor into securing a mortgage loan?

A: A lower interest rate allows you to borrow more money than a high rate with the same monthly payment. It also means you'll be paying less for the privilege of using their money. Remember, interest rates go up and down quickly, so ask lenders if they offer a rate "lock-in," which will guarantee you a specific interest rate for a certain period of time.

Q: What causes interest rates to change constantly?

A: Interest rates change due to a number of factors, and it is hard to predict in which direction they will go. The Federal Reserve from time to time raises or lowers its prime lending rate to control inflation. This fluctuation causes banks to raise and lower their rates, and then mortgage rates tend to go up and down.

The rule of supply and demand also plays a part in the ups and downs in interest rates. If there is a demand for mortgages, interest rates have a tendency to rise. Higher rates, however, tend to slow down perspective buyers from shopping. When the market starts to feel the effects brought on by the higher interest rates, rates have a tendency to drop. This is true for the overall economy as well. If the economic climate is slow, consumers and businesses tend to borrow less and the rates go down. If the economy is good, the rates tend to move up.

The U.S. bond market also plays a part in the yo-yoing of interest rates. Lenders use detailed formulas to help develop interest rates from the performance of the U.S. bond market.

The key factor to remember is that rates vary. If rates are high, don't always assume that they'll keep climbing. History seems to imply that what goes up, must come down. Shop around to get the best rate for your mortgage. It will not hurt to let the lenders know that you are shopping around. Even lenders are known to be competitive.

Q: How do I decide which loan will be best for me?

A: Your personal situation will determine the best kind of loan for you. But to determine exactly what your situation is and to help start narrowing your search among the many different types of loans, you can ask yourself a few questions:

- Do I expect my finances to change over the next few years?
- Am I planning on living in the home for a long time? Or do I foresee eventually moving out of state or buying a bigger home to accommodate my growing family?
- Am I comfortable with the idea of a fluctuating monthly mortgage payment?
- Do I wish to be free of mortgage payments as my children approach college age or as I prepare for retirement?
- Do I have money saved for a down payment?

The answers to these questions will help you see the advantages and disadvantages of each loan type and its options. Also, when you present these answers to your lender, he or she will be better able to assist you in deciding which loan best fits your needs.

Q: Are there special mortgages for first-time home-buyers?

A: Yes. Lenders now offer several affordable mortgage options that help first-time buyers over hurdles that made purchasing a home difficult in the past. Today's lenders may be able to help borrowers with little or no down payment, those who have no or a less-than-shining credit history, those who have quite a bit of long-term debt, and even those who have experienced a fluctuating income source.

The best advice is to do your own research on the different types of loans and then go to several lenders and ask about any options you may have overlooked.

Q: What is a conventional loan?

A: Conventional loans are loans that are not government insured or guaranteed like the FHA or VA loans. They are issued by private lenders and, in most cases, allow loan amounts of 80 percent of the value of the property.

Q: What are the advantages of opting for a fifteen-year loan versus the traditional thirty-year loan?

A: Other than outright owning your home in half the time, fifteen-year loans offer lots of appeal for those who can afford them. Imagine building your equity faster and saving thousands of dollars in finance charges. While it is true that fif-teen-year loans may be harder to secure because you will need a higher income, many homebuyers assume that because the loan is paid off in half the time, the payments will automatically be double those of a thirty-year mortgage. This assumption is wrong. Because more of the monthly payment goes toward principal and less toward interest, fifteen-year loans usually increase only 20 to 30 percent. For example, with a $150,000 loan, you could pay it off at 6.75 percent in thirty years at $973 a month, with interest costs of $200,243. Or you could borrow the same amount at 6.5 percent with a fifteen-year loan and pay $1,307 a month, with total interest costs of only $85,199.

Q: What is a fixed-rate loan?

A: A fixed-rate loan or mortgage is one in which the total sum of the interest and principal stays the same for the life of the loan. In other words, the amount you agree to pay monthly will not increase, even if there is a rise in interest rates.

In most cases, a fixed-rate loan is set for a period of fif-teen or thirty years. It bears mentioning, however, that while your interest rate and principle will not change, your total payment may go up if the mortgage company or bank also pays the insurance and taxes through escrow. It is very likely that insurance and taxes will fluctuate from year to year.

Q: What are the advantages and disadvantages of a fixed-rate loan?

A: Because most people like to know exactly what their monthly debt will be, and because people feel they can always refinance if interest rates drop, a fixed-rate loan is the most traditional of mortgages and considered by many to be the most advantageous. However, because interest rates and mortgage options change often, and because each type of mortgage comes with its own advantages and disadvantages, the loan that may benefit you will depend on your particular circumstances.

The biggest advantage of a fixed-rate mortgage is that you will pay significantly less interest over the life of the loan. Therefore, this is probably the best option for those who foresee living in the home for many years. Unless you are buying at a time with very high interest rates, rates for the next three to ten years are more apt to go up than down. Considering this, getting tied into a fixed rate is generally good advice.

Many homebuyers see going with a loan with adjustable interest rates as a gamble. However, fixed loans are generally known to come with higher interest rates, making some of the alternative mortgages tempting. Mortgages with adjustable-rate interest can help buyers keep monthly housing costs down for the first few years, and oftentimes buyers will be likely to pay less money up front.

Q: If I go with a fixed rate, what happens if interest rates decrease?

A: If interest rates drop significantly after you've secured your loan, you may want to investigate refinancing. Most experts agree that if you plan to be in your house for at least eighteen months and you get a rate 2 percent lower than your current one, refinancing is a smart move.

Q: What is a balloon mortgage?

A: A balloon mortgage starts off like a normal fixed-rate loan in that you agree to make a fixed monthly payment. While your payment may be figured based on a thirty-year loan, you are agreeing that, after a predetermined time (usually three to seven years), you will either pay off the remaining debt or apply for another loan. In some instances a fixed-rate with a balloon option may come with a lower interest rate, which is appealing to home-buyers. Keep in mind that if your finances or credit deteriorate, it may be difficult to get the lender to refinance. And when it is time to refinance, you may have to settle with higher interest rates than you could have received at the initial purchase.

Q: When should I consider a balloon mortgage and when is it not a good idea?

A: If you are certain to move due to a career transfer or if you foresee needing a bigger home due to needed space to raise a family, a balloon mortgage may be for you. Because a balloon mortgage may come with a lower interest rate, it could be advantageous to someone about to come into a large amount of money, such as a trust or inheritance.

On the flip side, if you are considering taking a balloon mortgage solely because of the lower interest rate, are you really prepared to come up with the remaining balance when the balloon payment comes due? The question deserves careful consideration because you could be at risk of losing the property.

Q: What is an adjustable-rate mortgage?

A: Unlike fixed-rate loans, adjustable-rate mortgages (ARMs) are mortgages that have interest rates that change during the life of the loan. In most cases, ARMs offer a starting low interest rate that can be three or more percentage points lower than a fixed-rate loan. Professionals often refer to the ARMs' beginning low interest rate as a "teaser" rate, offering a clue to homebuyers that the interest rates are destined to go up. Variations of ARMs are available. (See page 82 for information on hybrids.)

Q: What makes an ARM's interest rate go up and down?

A: The rates fluctuate due to changes in the economy. There are various ways to interpret the state of the economy and different ways to figure how the ups and downs of the economy will affect an ARM's interest rate. One of those ways is to look at the index to which your ARM is linked.

Q: What is an index, and is one index better than another?

A: An index is basically a set of factors with which the economy and interest rates are measured. There are many choices of indexes, carrying a variety of components, meaning each index may use different factors to decide if your rate will go up or down.

Indexes are more often chosen by the lender and not the homebuyer, yet there are a few lenders who offer the borrower a choice. If you have a preference for one index over another, you can shop around until you find a lender offering the index you prefer.

Just as different loans come with advantages and disadvantages, so do indexes. Your best choice in indexes is one that is considered less volatile, meaning an index that is least vulnerable to frequent or major swings in interest rates. But like loans, the indexes that offer the overall best rates are those that tend to be more vulnerable to changes in the economy. The trick is finding one that offers the best rate and has the least volatility. Also to be considered is the term of the index. For example, an ARM pegged to a six-month U.S. Treasury bill index is more volatile than one with a one-year index. The longer the term of the index, the more the borrower is protected from short-term interest-rate fluctuations.

One of the more common indexes is the one-year Treasury securities (known as T-bills). T-bills come with a higher rate but are less likely to fluctuate. Two other popular options that are often lower but more volatile are the London InterBank Offering Rate (LIBOR) and the slightly higher, but less volatile, Cost of Funds Index for Western banks in the Federal Reserve's Eleventh District.

While the *Wall Street Journal* prints most of the index rates, you can ask your lender where else you can look for information and figures on the indexes it uses. However, before you get too involved in index comparing, it is best to remember that there are no clear-cut winners.

Q: What are the advantages and disadvantages of an ARM mortgage?

A: Obviously, lower interest rates that translate into lower monthly payments for the first few years make ARM mortgages attractive. Borrowers who are risk takers at heart and are willing to sacrifice the long-term security of a fixed-rate loan find themselves leaning toward this mortgage. This isn't to say that ARMs are always considered too risky, or that they aren't beneficial in some circumstances. There are two good reasons to choose an ARM: if you expect to move within five years, or if you want or need the lower rate to help you qualify for the loan that puts you into your dream house.

If you are choosing an ARM because the lower payment is all you can afford, a good question to consider is if you truly see your financial picture improving in the near future. Perhaps you, or your spouse, are about to graduate from college or maybe you are next in line for a promotion at work, and the chance of a large increase in your income is almost guaranteed. While it still may be risky to predict your income, there are some risks worth taking. That said, it is always wise to consider the worst-case scenario. Before you decide on this type of loan, ask your loan officer to explain exactly how high your monthly payments could climb. In some of the extreme cases where interest rates have sky-rocketed, homeowners have seen their interest rates double over a short period of time, which could almost double your payments.

Q: What are the questions I should ask the loan officer before choosing an ARM?

A: Below are questions consumers should ask their loan officer before choosing an ARM:

- How long will the initial interest rate remain in effect?
- What will the interest rate be after the first adjustment?

- How high can the interest rate go if interest rates continue to rise?
- How long will it take for the rate on the ARM to reach the maximum allowed under the loan program?
- Can I pay off the loan without having to pay penalties?

Q: What is an adjustable-rate cap?

A: An adjustable-rate cap is a limit on increases and decreases of the interest rates pertaining to this type of loan. In addition to restrictions on how high and how low the interest rates can go over the length of the mortgage, most caps also include how high the rates can be adjusted at one given time.

A typical structure of an ARM cap includes a 2-percentage-point cap on annual increases, with a 6-percentage-point cap over the life of the mortgage. If you begin with a 6 percent loan, it could go up in 2 percent increments per year to 8 percent, 10 percent, 12 percent. This means you could go to paying double the interest in three years. Understanding exactly how your ARM cap works is important.

Q: What is an adjustment interval, and how soon and how often does it fluctuate?

A: An adjustment interval is the frequency with which your rate can be changed. Generally, adjustment intervals begin adjusting after the first year and are commonly adjusted every year after that. But homebuyers should never make assumptions. Your adjustment interval should be clearly spelled out in your mortgage agreement. Some are set to change every six months, and others can be found that adjust every three years. Different lenders will offer different adjustment intervals.

In some cases, a mortgage that adjusts twice a year may come with a lower start rate than one that is adjusted only once a year. Before opting for the shorter interval period, consider that a once-a-year interval may allow you time to prepare for the increase in the monthly payment, where a six-month interval may be difficult to handle.

Q: What are hybrid loans?

A: Hybrid loans are mortgages that, at a predetermined time, are converted to a different loan type. This change will generally alter the way you repay the debt. For example, balloon mortgages, loans that start out as fixed-rate but come due for payoff in five to ten years, are hybrids. Other forms of hybrids may be fixed-rate loans that are set to change over to variable-rate mortgages.

Hybrid loans have lower rates than fixed-rate loans, but they come with the risk of having the monthly payments increase substantially due to a rise in interest rates. Homebuyers who need a little wiggle room on the rate to qualify for the loan, or who expect to move before the fixed-rate part of the loan expires are good candidates for hybrid loans.

Q: What are low-doc or no-doc loans?

A: Doc stands for documentation. A low-doc lender will consider you for a home loan without seeing a lot of the documentation, such as tax returns, business statements, and other paperwork, that a normal lender would require. However, the one thing even a low-doc lender will probably review is your credit.

Homebuyers who have complicated financial situations or those who are self-employed may find these loans an option. Generally, people who are in a hurry to get into a particular home or people whose income is rapidly increasing are good candidates for this type of loan. However, the no-hassle approach of approval comes at a price. Most low-doc and no-doc loans charge over-the-top interest rates.

Q: What are prepayment penalties?

A: Some adjustable mortgage agreements put clauses into the contract that allow them to charge you a penalty if you decide to pay off the loan or to pay off a large portion of the loan. Most prepayment penalties are often negotiable. If possible, ask for no prepayment penalty or for the lowest one possible.

Q: Is the lowest interest rate always the best?

A: A low rate is important, but you need to look at all the terms of the loan in light of your personal situation. The lower rate may require you to pay a number of discount points and or origination fees. (For more information on discount points, see pages 59 and 159.)

Both discount points and origination fees are prepaid interest; therefore, if you are having trouble coming up with a down payment, they can add to the financial problem.

In some cases, the reduction in interest rates is not enough to justify the amount of the discount points or origination fees. While lower rates usually mean the best deal over the long term, not everyone is looking at the long-term benefits.

Going with the lowest-rate loan may not be the most beneficial option if you're not planning on owning the home for a long period of time. A good lender will be able to show you the long-term savings of low interest rates and, depending on your plans of selling or moving, when it might be advantageous to go with a higher rate.

Q: What is an escrow account and do I need one?

A: Set up by your lender, an escrow account is a place to set aside a portion of your monthly payment to cover annual charges for homeowner's insurance, mortgage insurance (if applicable), and property taxes.

In general, escrow accounts are a good idea because they guarantee that the money will always be available for these payments, which can often be unexpected. If you decide to go with an escrow account that pays property taxes or homeowner's insurance, make sure the lender, and not you, is required to pay penalties on late payments because the lender will be the one responsible for making the payments.

Q: What is private mortgage insurance (PMI)?

A: Private mortgage insurance (PMI) is insurance to protect the lender in case you, the buyer, default on the loan.

Most lenders require PMI when the down payment is less than 20 percent of the cost of the property. For some first-time buyers, PMI is one of those unexpected expenses of buying a house.

With the exception of some government and older loans, once you have owned your home for a few years, and your equity reaches a certain percentage, usually 22 percent, you are entitled to cancel your PMI policy. However, the lender will not notify you of this. You are required to contact the lender and request that the insurance be canceled. Many homeowners throw away hundreds of dollars paying for PMI when it is no longer needed. To avoid this, ask your lender for an approximate date on which you can cancel the PMI policy.

Q: How much does PMI cost?

A: While PMI rates vary from one insurance lender to another, it is generally not too costly. In most cases, it is paid monthly and runs around one-half of 1 percent of the mortgage loan. For a $100,000 mortgage, the PMI would be approximately $20 per month.

Some lenders now offer their own PMI insurance at lower costs. Ask about your options at the time of approval.

Q: Is there any way to avoid paying PMI?

A: Normally, if you're putting down 20 percent or more of your mortgage, you won't need to pay PMI. If you have good credit, you may be able to get a separate down payment loan so you can avoid paying PMI, but you should look seriously at the financial benefits of borrowing because this may cause your mortgage loan to have a slightly higher interest rate and higher loan fees.

Q: Because of my lack of credit, I was told I might need a cosigner—exactly what is a cosigner?

A: A cosigner is a person who pledges in writing as part of the credit contract to repay the debt if the borrower fails to do so. The cosigner's credit will be reviewed and must pass the lender's evaluation as well. It is also wise to remember that the account will be displayed on the credit report of the cosigner just as it will appear on the borrower's credit report.

Q: What is the U.S. Department of Housing and Urban Development?

A: Also known as HUD, this organization was established in 1965 to develop national policies and programs to address overall housing needs in the United States. Their mission was, and is, to create a suitable living environment for all Americans by developing and improving the country's communities through forming and enforcing fair housing laws.

Q: How does HUD assist homebuyers and homeowners?

A: HUD provides assistance to consumers by setting forth a variety of programs that develop and support affordable housing. HUD plays a huge part in helping people achieve their dreams of owning a home by making loans obtainable for lower- and moderate-income families through its FHA mortgage insurance program and the HUD Homes Program. HUD owns homes in numerous communities across America and markets them at attractive prices that come with economical terms. In addition, HUD seeks to protect consumers by providing a vast amount of education, enforcing Fair Housing Laws, and offering housing rehabilitation initiatives.

Q: How can I get listings of HUD homes for sale?

A: You can see lists of available HUD homes on its Web site: *www.hud.gov.* You can even get directions to the properties that interest you, see maps, as well as get information about local schools in the home's area. At HUD's site you will also find a link to other homes being sold by federal agencies.

Q: If I am interested in a HUD home, what do I do?

A: If you find a home that interests you, you will need to contact a HUD-approved real estate broker (most brokers are HUD approved) and request that he or she submit a bid for you. Successful bids are posted on the page for your state.

Q: I am a teacher and I've heard of the program TND (Teacher Next Door). What is it?

A: In its quest to make American communities stronger, the U.S. Department of Housing and Urban Development designed this program to encourage teachers to buy homes in low- and moderate-income neighborhoods.

The TND program offers an amazing financial benefit for applicants. Properties are offered to teachers at a 50 percent discount. To make a HUD home even more affordable, participants can apply for an FHA-assured mortgage with a down payment of only $100, and they can finance all closing costs. If the TND home needs repairs, HUD offers the 203(k) loan, which allows the homebuyer to finance both the purchase of the home and the cost of needed repairs.

Q: Can I qualify to participate in the TND program?

A: According to HUD, the TND program is open to anyone employed full time by a public school; private school; or federal, state, county, or municipal education agency as a state-certified classroom teacher or administrator in grades K–12.

To qualify for this program, teachers must be in good standing with their employers and be employed in the district/jurisdiction in which the TND home is located. Participants do not have to be a first-time homebuyer, but they cannot own another home at the closing time of the TND home. Applicants must also agree to live in the HUD home as their main residence for three years.

Q: How is a TND property sold?

A: TND homes are listed and sold exclusively over the Internet. To see if any homes are available in your area, go to the Web site (*www.hud.gov*). The TND listings can be found in the Revitalization Area section and are marked with a special Teacher Next Door button. You can check out availability of homes in your area by logging in your zip code. Bids are awarded only once a week, and your bid must be the amount of the list price. Interested parties can submit their own bid or have a real estate broker assist them. The winning bid is selected randomly by a computer and is posted each week on the same Web address.

For more information about the TND program, contact your local HUD Homeownership Center, log on to *www.hud.gov*, or obtain information on the HELP line at 1-800-569-4287.

Q: What is the Officer Next Door program?

A: Almost exactly like the TND program, the Officer Next Door (OND) is another HUD program specifically for sworn law enforcement officers who are employed full time by federal, state, county, or municipal government, or by a public or private college or university.

The requirements and benefits for this program are the same as those listed above for the TND program. For more information about the OND, contact your local HUD Homeownership Center, log on to *www.hud.gov*, or see information on the HELP line at 1-800-569-4287.

Q: How can I get more information about HUD and its programs?

A: More information can be found at a HUD office. Look in the phone book for a listing of the HUD agency closest to you. You can also go to HUD's Web site at *www.hud.gov*.

Q: What is the federal Farmers Home Administration (FmHA) and how can it help me become a homeowner?

A: If you are looking to buy a home in a rural area, the FmHA offers no-down-payment programs and lower-than-market interest rates. There are some stipulations. The house you buy must meet their definition of rural, and it must be your principal residence and not just a second, country home. To get more information, contact the Farmers Home Administration, which is a part of the U.S. Department of Agriculture, at the Web site *www.rurdev.usda.gov.*

Q: What is Fannie Mae?

A: Fannie Mae, the Federal National Mortgage Association, is basically what people call secondary lenders. They lend to the institutions that lend to you. They provide home-buying information, guidelines for mortgage qualification, and applications for low-down-payment mortgages. To get more information about their programs, log on to *www. fanniemae.com* or call 1-202-752-7000.

Q: Is Freddie Mac the same as Fannie Mae?

A: While often confused, these are two different lending institutions. Like Fannie Mae, Freddie Mac is a secondary lender and offers some low-down-payment mortgages. For information about Freddie Mac, log on to *www.freddiemac. com* or refer to your phone book for the closest Freddie Mac headquarters.

Q: What is the FHA?

A: The Federal Housing Administration (FHA) was established in 1934 to advance and promote opportunities for Americans to own homes. Now an agency within HUD, the FHA provides private lenders with mortgage insurance. This program offers the security the lenders need to be able to offer loans to buyers who may not be able to apply for a conventional loan. Generally speaking, FHA loans may not have the best interest rates, but thanks to their availability, more than 26 million Americans have attained their dream of owning a home.

Years ago, getting FHA financing was a long-drawn-out process. Today, the process has been streamlined, making it easier and quicker. Some people even say securing an FHA loan can be quicker than securing a conventional loan.

Q: Exactly how can FHA help me buy a house?

A: The FHA allows thousands of people yearly to attain home loans—people who may have been turned down otherwise. Basically, by guaranteeing to pay the lenders if the homebuyer defaults on the loan, the FHA removes the risk from the lenders, thus allowing lenders to loan to consumers with no credit or less-than-shining credit.

The FHA can also assist you by providing loan options with lower down payments than conventional loans. In some cases, an FHA down payment can be as little as the first and last month's rent required to move into an apartment. And, depending on your financial situation, your monthly payments could be comparable to an average rental amount.

Q: How is the FHA funded?

A: Lender claims paid by the FHA mortgage insurance programs are acquired from the Mutual Mortgage Insurance fund. This account is made up of premiums paid by FHA-insured loan borrowers. No tax dollars are used to fund the FHA.

Q: Can I qualify for an FHA loan?

A: Anyone who meets the credit requirements (which are not as strenuous as those of conventional loans), who can afford the mortgage payments, who has the finances for the down payment/closing costs, and who plans to use the mortgaged home as a primary residence may apply for an FHA-insured loan.

Q: Is there a loan limit for FHA loans?

A: Yes, there is a loan limit but it varies throughout the country. It can range from $115,200 in a low-cost area to $208,800 in higher-cost areas. The loan maximums go higher for multiunit homes. Because maximums are figured by the conforming loan limit and the average home price in the area, the FHA loan limits do fluctuate. It is best to ask your lender for details of current limits in your area.

Q: What steps are involved in getting an FHA loan?

A: For the most part, applying for an FHA home loan is the same as applying for a conventional loan. (See pages 61–69 to learn about applying for a loan.) The difference is the FHA process may require the completion of more forms. With some new automation measures now in place, securing an FHA loan is easier and quicker. For those people who do not want a face-to-face meeting, the FHA now allows you to apply for a loan via mail, telephone, the Internet, or video conference.

Q: Do I make enough money to qualify for an FHA loan?

A: FHA loans were designed for low-income homebuyers. There is no minimum income requirement. However, you must prove regular income for at least three years and have a measurably good credit report showing you have consistently paid your bills on time.

Q: Is there a debt-to-income ratio for FHA loans?

A: Yes. The FHA allows you to use 29 percent of your income toward housing costs (mortgage payments) and 41 percent toward housing expenses (monthly bills) and other long-term debt. However, there are circumstances that may alter the numbers. (See below for information about exceeding the debt ratio.)

When thinking about debt-to-income ratio, you should realize that child support, retirement pensions, unemployment compensations, VA benefits, military pay, Social Security income, alimony, and seasonal pay are considered income. If proved as a steady source, overtime and part-time pay and even bonuses will be viewed as income. Where FHA is concerned, the source of money is not as important as the steadiness of the income.

Q: How does the debt-to-income ratio for FHA compare to the debt-to-income ratios of conventional loans?

A: Because the FHA was designed for lower-income families, it makes sense that the debt-to-income ratio of FHA loans would allow a slightly higher debt ratio. Generally speaking, conventional loans allow only 28 percent toward housing costs and 36 percent toward housing expenses and other debt.

Q: Is there any way to exceed the debt-to-income ratio with FHA loans?

A: There are several circumstances that may allow you to exceed the debt-to-income ratio.

- A large down payment
- Substantial cash reserves
- A demonstrated ability to pay a higher percentage of income toward your housing expenses
- Evidence of good credit history or limited credit use
- Having a net worth that is enough to repay the mortgage regardless of income
- A decrease in monthly housing expenses
- Acquiring a less-than-maximum mortgage term
- Funds provided by an organization

Q: Exactly how much of a down payment do I need to get an FHA loan?

A: The most affordable FHA loan programs offered by private lenders require between a 3 percent and 5 percent down payment. There is a prerequisite that 3 percent of the down payment come directly from the borrower's own funds.

Q: What kind of financial resources can I use for the down payment and closing costs of an FHA loan?

A: As with conventional loans, you can use cash gifts as well as money from a private savings club such as a 401(k). However, if you can do certain repairs and improvements yourself, your labor, referred to as "sweat equity," can account for as much as 8 percent of your down payment.

Q: Is FHA generally more flexible than conventional lenders when it comes to reviewing credit history?

A: Yes, FHA is considerably more flexible when reviewing credit. People with no or little credit will usually find it easier to secure an FHA loan. As for those with poor credit history, with an FHA loan you can most likely establish credit if:

- Two years have passed since a bankruptcy has been discharged
- Any outstanding tax liens have been repaid or the proper arrangements have been made to set up a repayment plan with a state Department of Revenue or the IRS
- All outstanding judgments have been paid
- At least three years have passed since a foreclosure or a deed-in-lieu has been resolved

Q: What are the closing costs with an FHA-insured loan?

A: The closing costs associated with an FHA loan are comparable to those of a conventional loan with one exception: the FHA requires an upfront mortgage insurance premium equal to 2.25 percent of the mortgage to be paid at closing. If the homebuyer meets the requirement of having completed the Homebuyer Education Learning Program (HELP), he or she can get a lower rate of 1.75 percent. This premium may be partially refunded if the loan is paid in full during the first seven years of the loan term.

If your mortgage is more than fifteen years or if you have a loan with an LTV greater than 90 percent, you will be required to pay an annual premium, which is divided over twelve months and figured into monthly payments. (For more information about closing costs, see the "Closing and Contract Facts" section.)

Q: Can I have my FHA closing costs figured into my loan amount?

A: No. FHA closing costs cannot be rolled into the loan. However, you may be able to use the amount you pay for them as part of your down payment. Ask your lender for specific details.

Q: Can I assume an FHA loan?

A: Yes. FHA loans are assumable and can be very beneficial to someone wanting to avoid some of the initial costs of home-buying. Assuming a loan can also result in the homebuyer's getting a lower interest rate. There is no property appraisal requirement, and other than a credit check, where you must meet regular FHA standards, the process is considered streamlined and is less expensive than that of acquiring a new loan.

Q: What is the FHA HELP program?

A: The Homebuyer Education Learning Program (HELP) is a structured program designed to assist low-income families who need extra assistance achieving their dreams of owning a home. Topics covered in the program include: budgeting, finding a home, getting a loan, and home maintenance. Parties who complete the program are generally entitled to a reduction in the initial FHA mortgage insurance premium from the required 2.25 percent to 1.75 percent of the total purchase price of the new home.

Q: Will I be required to get mortgage insurance with an FHA loan?

A: Yes. Just as with a conventional loan, if your down payment is less than 20 percent of the cost of your home, you will be required to get mortgage insurance.

Q: What is the FHA 203(b) loan?

A: The 203(b) loan is the most commonly used FHA loan program. Its plan includes a low down payment, flexible qualifying guidelines, limited lender's fees, and a maximum loan amount.

Q: Which FHA program should I look to if I am planning to purchase a fixer-upper?

A: The 203(k) loan. This plan enables you to borrow both the sale price for the house and its renovation loan. The loan amount offered is based on the estimated postrefurbishment value of the house.

The maximum amount you can borrow for renovations is subject to FHA lending guidelines set for your particular geographic area. Financing is based on an estimate of the value of the home after renovations. The loan is then given for the amount of the house and repair costs. Interest rates may be a little higher than conventional mortgage rates, but they are normally lower than rates given for conventional renovation loans. There is a minimum of $5,000, but generally, almost all fixer-uppers will meet this repair quota. The money can even be spent on paint, sod, and appliances.

Q: What is a Title 1 loan?

A: The Title 1 loan is another option for those buying a fixer-upper. However, this particular loan doesn't include the price of the mortgage. The FHA insures loans up to $25,000 to be used to make nonluxury renovation and repairs to a home. The payback period can be as long as twenty years. Interest charged might be higher than with home-equity loans, but it is generally lower than with a home-improvement loan from a commercial lender, and the interest is tax deductible.

Below are some advantages of the Title 1 program:

- You do not have to live in any particular area to secure one of these loans.

- You seldom need any security for loans under $7,500, other than your signature on a note, and you don't need a cosigner.
- You need only to own the property (or have a long-term lease on it), fill out a loan application that shows you are a good credit risk, and execute a note agreeing to repay the loan.
- You do not have to disturb any mortgage or deed of trust you have on your home.
- Your loan can cover architectural and engineering costs, building permit fees, title examination costs, appraisal fees, and inspection fees.

Q: What is an energy efficient mortgage (EEM)?

A: The Energy Efficient Mortgage (EEM) is a loan designed to help homebuyers save future money on utility costs. Basically, the cost of adding energy-efficiency features is figured into the cost of a home. Both the 203(b) and the 203(k) can be joined with an EEM. Below are guidelines for EEMs:

- The cost of improvements must be determined by an energy consultant or a Home Energy Rating System. This cost must be less than the anticipated saving from the improvements.
- One/two-unit new or existing homes are eligible. Condos are not included in this plan.
- The improvements financed may be 5 percent of the property value or $4,000, whichever is higher. The sum financed must fall within the FHA loan limit.

Q: What other programs or loan products does FHA offer the consumer?

A: FHA programs include insuring loans for the purchase of rehabilitation of manufactured homes, cooperatives, and condominiums. They provide special programs for urban areas, disaster victims, and members of the armed forces. Also provided by FHA is insurance for ARMs.

Q: Where can I go to obtain an FHA-insured loan?

A: Any mortgage company, bank, or savings and loan association that is FHA approved (most are) can assist you in getting an FHA loan. For more information on the FHA, visit *www.hud.gov* or call a HUD-approved counseling agency at 1-800-569-4287.

Q: What is a VA guaranteed home loan?

A: A VA guaranteed loan is made by private lenders such as savings and loans, mortgage companies, or banks to eligible veterans who are buying a home that will serve as their main residence. Just as the FHA assures the lender that it will be paid if the homeowner defaults, so does the VA.

While VA loans allow the borrower to make a lower down payment, they also may come with more restrictions than a standard bank loan does. (These restrictions change and are updated frequently, so check with the VA before applying.) Generally speaking, veterans can get into a home with a lower investment, the interest rates are negotiable, there are no mortgage insurance premiums, and the loan has no prepay penalty.

A VA fee is required by law. The fee is currently 2 percent on no-down-payment loans. (Fees do change, and it is recommended that an interested participant check with his or her lenders or the U.S. Department of Veterans Affairs for updates.) The funding for second-time users for the no-down-payment loan is 3 percent. If the homebuyer chooses to provide a down payment, the fee is decreased.

One should also know that being eligible for a VA loan doesn't guarantee a loan. Your credit history and income still must pass the lender's qualifications.

Q: Are all veterans eligible for a VA loan?

A: The Veterans Administration has specific guidelines for qualification. To see if you meet those requirements, log on to *www.homeloans.va.gov* or look in the Yellow Pages for the closest U.S. Department of Veterans Affairs.

Q: Am I limited to only one VA loan?

A: No, you are not limited to one loan. However, your eligibility is dependent on your circumstances. If you have paid off the old VA loan and no longer have the property, or, on a one-time-only basis, if your old loan is paid and you still own the property, you may be able to be approved. In either case, to obtain restoration of eligibility, the veteran must send the administration a completed VA form 26-1880 with evidence that the former loan has been paid in full.

Q: Can I build a new home with a VA loan?

A: Although they are allowed by law, most lenders do not offer construction loans. Once a home is completed, an applicant can apply for a VA loan to refinance a construction loan.

Q: How much is my VA entitlement?

A: The basic entitlement is $36,000 (or up to $60,000 for loans over $144,000). Lenders will generally lend up to four times your available entitlement without requiring a down payment. This condition is contingent on your income, credit history, and if the property appraises for the asking price.

Q: What is my maximum VA loan limit?

A: There is no maximum limit with VA loans, but lenders generally will not exceed $240,000. The reason is because many veterans sell their loans, and if the new owners default, the loan is insured only for the $240,000.

Q: How do I apply for a VA guaranteed loan?

A: Applying for a VA loan is the same as applying for most loans, with a few exceptions. When you sign a purchase contract, put a contingency into the contract that the purchase is conditioned on the approval of your "VA" home loan. Also, when you apply for a loan, make sure you have a Certificate of Eligibility.

The lender will then ask the VA to assign a licensed appraiser to determine the reasonable value of the property. The lender will let you know the decision on the loan. The process could take one to six weeks.

Q: How do I get a Certificate of Eligibility?

A: To get your Certificate of Eligibility, submit a completed VA Form 26-1880. You can also request the Certificate at one of the VA Eligibility Centers, but make sure you bring proof of military service.

Some lenders have access to the ACE (automated Certificate of Eligibility) and it may be possible to obtain a Certificate of Eligibility from your lender in only a matter of seconds. However, not all cases can be processed through ACE. Call and ask your lender before applying.

Q: How does the closing cost of a VA loan compare to that of conventional loans?

A: Closing costs are comparable with other financing types and may even be lower.

Q: What is the VA prepurchase counseling?

A: Prepurchase counseling is a great source of education offered by the VA. The information covers the process of buying a home, the key players in the homebuying process, and debt management. The goal is to create more informed homebuyers better prepared to meet their responsibilities.

While the counseling is not required, it is recommended. The counseling is usually free.

Q: Can I get a VA loan if I have filed for bankruptcy in the last few years?

A: A bankruptcy on your credit report does not automatically disqualify you from acquiring a loan. Below are some basic rules that apply:

- If the bankruptcy was discharged more than two years ago, it may be disregarded.
- If the bankruptcy was discharged within the last one to two years, the loan may be contingent on your more recent credit history and perhaps the circumstances surrounding the bankruptcy, for example, unemployment or serious illness.
- Applications with bankruptcy within the past twelve months are generally determined to be unsatisfactory.

Part Three

Shopping for a Home

You have decided to buy; you have found your agent and know how the agent and buyer's relationship works. You've secured your loan, and now it is time for the fun part—the actual shopping. Notice I said fun, not easy. Not only will finding a home require lots of legwork, but during this part of the home-buying process, you're going to need all your wits. There are a lot of questions you'll need to ask, a lot of questions you'll need to answer, and a lot of decisions to be made. While shopping is seen as the fun part, this is also the time you may be faced with disappointments. You may find a home you love, only to discover it's in a neighborhood you can't accept. Then you may fall for a neighborhood, only to discover the house is in need of too many repairs.

In this section, the questions will cover everything from checking out a neighborhood to knowing the pros and cons of buying particular types of homes—a fixer-upper versus a new home, a condo versus a patio home. You'll find questions on the most common defects of homes, and the right questions to ask about homeowners associations. The goal of this chapter is to make you a wiser consumer and help you choose the best possible house in the best possible location.

Q: How does one evaluate a neighborhood?

A: One person's idea of the perfect neighborhood may vary considerably from another's. However, there are some general rules of thumb for evaluating locations and neighborhoods. Below is a list of things to consider about neighborhoods and how to investigate the issues before you seriously considering buying.

Good Schools

You should check test scores, classroom sizes, and the crime rate in the schools. While people with children are generally good about checking out the education system, even those without children should consider doing so. In addition to finding out about the local school taxes, you would be wise to learn about the quality of the local school because a bad school may mean the declining of the neighborhood and will definitely affect the property value. To get information about the local schools, you can go to the schools for a tour, contact the local chamber of commerce, or log on to one of these Web sites: *www.Realtor.com, www.Monster moving.monster.com,* or *www.houseandhome.com.* Be aware of some of the signs that a school may be in decline. Some signs to watch for are dropping test scores, dropping student enrollment, poorly maintained or vandalized buildings, and trouble at the PTA meetings.

Low Crime Rates

How many robberies have taken place in the neighborhood? Is car theft a problem in the general vicinity? You can get this information from the local police's public affairs department. Some chamber Web sites also make crime-rate information available. Crime-rate information can also be found on the same Web sites mentioned above.

A Well-Anchored and Established Area

Are there too many empty lots that could be sold to less-than-desirable commercial or industrial companies? Is there an excessive amount of homes in the area for sale or for rent? What do these homeowners know that you don't? Ask your agent who would be the best person to ask about any upcoming changes in the area. Don't be afraid to drop by local small businesses and ask the locals or visit with neighbors and ask questions about the neighborhood.

Pride of Ownership

Are the homes all well kept and the lawns manicured? Although we often center our focus on the home itself—its size, the extra-large garage, how our furniture will look perfect in the space—we shouldn't neglect to check out what's around the home. Imagine your friends and family driving into the neighborhood; is this a place you would be proud to live in? Before seriously considering a home, it is wise to walk around the neighborhood and really get a feel for the location. Don't be fooled by the scenic views as the agent takes you to and from the neighborhood; agents have a tendency to avoid any unpleasant areas.

Those Little Extras

Is there a park nearby? Does the neighborhood have lots of trees and wide streets and is it close to schools? Take several drives in the neighborhood to really get a good idea of what amenities this community offers.

Q: Where do I look for information on the property tax liability?

A: The total amount of the previous year's property taxes is normally included in the listing information. If it is not, request this information from your agent, or ask the seller for a tax receipt. You can also contact the local assessor's office. This is a good idea because tax rates can change from year to year.

Q: How many homes should I see before buying one?

A: It is possible that the first house you see could turn out to be the perfect home for you and your family. But how will you know if you don't continue looking? There isn't a set number of houses you should preview before you decide. You should visit as many homes as it takes to find the house that meets all your requirements or comes so close that you can't turn it down. However, on average, homebuyers see fifteen houses before making a purchase. Don't be afraid to remind your agent of the things you are looking for in a home if you feel you're not seeing homes that fit, or come close to fitting, into your ideals.

Q: Does the location of the home and lot placement in the neighborhood make a difference?

A: Yes. This should be considered for new and older homes. For the most part, it is always best to stay away from homes located on the outskirts of the neighborhood, for they may be more prone to sound pollution if the neighborhood backs up to a major thruway, and if the lots surrounding the home are not developed, you might wind up with an apartment overlooking your back patio. Also be aware of traffic patterns through a neighborhood. Is the house or lot you chose on the main street coming into or out of the neighborhood? Lots located on the edges of neighborhoods or on traffic-prone streets are generally less desirable.

Some people select a home depending on its location rather than on its style or size. For example, a home on a cul-de-sac with less traffic where the children can play dodge ball or a home located right down the street from the elementary school or the subdivision's park can hold more appeal than a home that has just the right floor plan or one that has the right color of brick. Choosing the right lot and location of a home will affect not only the quality of life you experience living in the home, but also the resale value of the property.

Q: What other concerns should I have about a neighborhood or an area before I buy?

A: We've heard about it and seen it on the national news—neighborhoods that are located in flood-prone areas, homes built on top of garbage dumps or near chemical plants that are now considered unsafe, communities where the water quality is below average. It is important to know what is beneath the grass on your property; to know if your area is prone to flooding; to know if an industrial plant in the area poses any health hazards; and to check out the services available in the area, such as water, sewer, and cable service.

The dirt beneath your home can affect the way your home settles over the years, and if you have a septic tank, it can mean the difference between a system that works and one that doesn't. In some developments built over the last twenty-five years, municipalities have required a "perc" or percolation test for property, which may tell the composition of the earth and will rate the ground absorption. To find out if the town you plan to buy into has a perc test, try contacting the builder inspector's office or the tax assessor's office.

Q: What is a FSBO?

A: FSBO (pronounced fizzbo) is a term meaning "for sale by owner."

Q: Since a FSBO is being sold without the costs of an agency/broker, can't I get more home for my money in a FSBO home?

A: In most cases, a seller who is attempting to sell his or her own property is doing so because he or she wants to maximize what he or she can get for the property. Whether or not that savings will be passed on to you is questionable. While a FSBO may sell in tight markets, statistically 80 to 90 percent of homeowners attempting to sell their own property wind up signing on with an agency. Also keep in mind that the average homeowner may not know the true value of the home's worth, and therefore the property could be overpriced. Don't take the word of a homeowner about the value of a home. Look at other homes that are for sale in the neighborhood.

Q: What happens if I find my dream home and it just happens to be a FSBO?

A: The answer seems simple: You buy it. First, however, you must ask yourself some serious questions. If you've signed contracts with a buyer's agent or broker, make sure you're not legally required to use their services even in the case of a FSBO home.

Next, ask yourself if you are prepared to make this deal without the help of someone who is trained in dealing with contracts, disclosures, and other legalities. Even if the owners are experienced in the selling process, is there any question where their loyalties will lie? It is wise to secure a professional to help you through the buying process. And who better to hire than a real estate agent/broker? If you are already working with one, have your agent contact the seller. If the seller is not willing to pay the commission, then you may offer to do so. Pay the broker 3 percent, or whatever commission he or she would have earned had they been working with the seller. If you are not yet working with an agent, finding a broker to work with you should not be hard. Since the home search is already complete, you may even be able to negotiate their fee.

Q: How can I find out about FSBOs?

A: You can look in the real estate ads in the local paper, but one of the best ways to find FSBOs is to first research neighborhoods where you think you would like to live and then drive around looking for signs. Call the number on the sign and make an appointment. It is not wise to just knock on the door and ask to see the home.

Q: Is an older home a better value than a new one?

A: This is a good question but it is hard to answer. While it is no secret that some older homes may be more affordable—especially when you're willing to consider the fixer-upper—the true answer depends on what you as a homeowner value. Basically, you should look at each home for its individual characteristics and see how it measures up according to your value system.

Older homes may be in more established neighborhoods, may offer more ambiance, and could have lower property-tax rates. Consumers who are looking at older homes, however, shouldn't mind the maintenance that comes with older homes, and they should expect to do some repairs.

Newer homes tend to have more modern architecture and systems and they are . . . new. They come with the new home smell; everything is shiny and clean. They are generally easier to maintain, and most will prove to be more energy efficient. People who purchase new homes usually don't want to worry, at least initially, about upkeep and repairs, and they typically want to be able to have more input in the overall design (choices in brick color, floor-plan layouts, flooring, paint colors, and window styles).

Q: What is a disclosure?

A: The word *disclosure* is likely to be referred to in two different areas when talking about real estate. In one sense of the word, real estate agents or brokers must "disclose" to the buyers that they represent the seller, because the seller will be paying them a fee for their services.

The other use of the word *disclosure* refers to the seller's, or agent/broker's, bringing any issues regarding the house to the attention of the buyers. Such issues may include whether the house has plumbing, electrical, foundation, or other problems. A disclosure could also contain any upcoming changes to the area the home is in or to the street it is on, or any new zoning regulations about to come into place. Normally, someone shopping for a home will not get the disclosure until he or she expresses serious interest in the home.

Q: How do I know the true value of a home?

A: One of the best ways to obtain information on what a property is worth is to ask your agent to see a list of comparable home sales in the area. Once you have this list, you can compare the houses on it to the houses you are interested in. Make sure to get the most recent sales figures because the market can fluctuate fast. And make sure that you look at similar houses in the same neighborhood to get a better understanding.

There are also Web sites that offer comparable sale prices on property. Both *www.homeradar.com* and *www.domania. com* list sale prices, dates of purchase, and addresses.

Q: Should I be concerned about the homeowners association?

A: A number of neighborhoods throughout the nation have formed homeowners associations that restrict certain activities on the property. These restrictions are designed to maintain property values and therefore are a positive thing. A good association fosters a sense of neighborliness and offers community parties and meetings.

However, all associations have certain covenants that you as a homeowner are required to follow. These rules may involve everything from having an RV parked in your driveway to having a basketball hoop in front of your home to the size of your pets. Some neighborhoods may even have a say in the color you paint your home. Another restriction often found in homeowners association policies is the rule of no home businesses. Some may consider babysitting a few children a home business. Some associations follow the rules exactly, and others are less likely to push issues.

It is important to understand the rules before you become serious about a home. Ask the association for its deed restrictions. These deed restrictions are also known as covenants, conditions, and restrictions, or CC&Rs.

Another reason to investigate the homeowners association is to be informed of any fees you must pay to the association. (Note that these fees, often called maintenance fees, cannot be claimed as a tax deduction.) It is important to know if the board that controls the association can raise these fees without a vote. Some can raise the fees 20 percent every year without a vote.

Q: Does a fixer-upper mean the seller will not pay for any repairs?

A: While the answer to this question may vary from seller to seller, generally, when a home is listed as a fixer-upper, the seller wants to sell the property without the added worry or costs of doing the repairs himself. However, depending on the type of mortgage you get, the home may or may not pass the lender's inspection and the sale is contingent on the seller's agreeing to do the needed repairs before the lender will approve the loan. If the seller really wants to sell the property, he or she may be willing to do some of the needed repairs. Fixer-uppers in need of major repairs may require a different type of loan. (See the "Loan Wisdom" section for information about the different types of loans.)

Q: When a home is referred to as a fixer-upper, how much fixing will it require?

A: A fixer-upper can be slightly shabby, or it can be a complete bomb. The best advice is to be honest with your agent about what conditions you feel you can handle and the conditions you want to avoid. For example, some homes in need of new flooring, paint, and perhaps a few knobs on the cabinets may be considered fixer-uppers. If you are looking for a good deal, you will probably be happy to consider a home that needs only a small face-lift.

However, a tumbledown shack and a home that has suffered a small fire or flood damage can also be qualified as fixer-uppers. Tell your agent your view of a fixer-upper and ask to be shown only those houses that fit into your ideals. However, remember that many times an agent will make a call to show you a home according to what is included in the MLS, and sometimes the defects of a home may be downplayed there.

Q: What are the advantages of buying a fixer-upper?

A: For those who enjoy rolling up their sleeves and love the smell of sawdust and fresh paint, a fixer-upper brings more than just financial benefits—it brings a sense of pride in having been part of the building process. There can be a number of advantages to buying a home that needs a little TLC (tender loving care). For many first-time buyers, a fixer-upper is the best option, and sometimes it is the only option. Shopping for a fixer-upper home can be compared to shopping for a new washing machine at a store that sells slightly dented appliances—the lower cost is one of the main attractions. Buying a fixer-upper is often a way for you to get into a better neighborhood that you couldn't otherwise afford. In some cases, fixer-uppers have been on the market a long time, and this also helps bring down the price. But you should also ask yourself if the other buyers know something that you don't. Perhaps the repairs the home needs are too costly to make.

Another advantage of buying a fixer-upper is that you may be able to buy more square footage for your money. If you are in the market for a larger home, but can afford only smaller home prices, consider looking at the homes in need of a face-lift. Because money may be short, be prepared to do the repairs in different stages. Maybe you can afford to redo the downstairs now and wait another year to get new carpet for the upstairs.

Another undeniable reason for choosing a home in need of repairs is that you can make some of the decorating decisions that you may not be able to make in a house that is move-in ready. You no longer have to hope to find a home with wallpaper in the dining room that will match your grandmother's china; you can choose the wallpaper yourself. From the color of the paint to the choice of flooring, you don't have to live with someone else's decorating taste for a few years. Buying a fixer-upper is one way to make sure your own personality is apparent in your home.

Q: What are the disadvantages of buying a fixer-upper?

A: As the name implies, the house is going to need fixing to bring it up to the average consumer's standards. And fixing requires money, work, and, oftentimes, the patience of a saint.

Ever heard a house referred to as a money pit? In most cases, it is the fixer-upper that earns this title. While the fixer-upper's lower price can make it appear to be a bargain, many homes in need of lots of repair have a tendency to cost the consumers more than they initially figured. You must be careful not to buy a home that is in such bad shape that it will cost more to repair than you could pay for a house in good condition in the same neighborhood.

Another thing to consider with the fixer-upper is that the condition of the house may limit you to certain loans. Some lenders will not finance a house that cannot become living quarters right away. (See the "Loan Wisdom" section for more information about loans.)

When considering buying a fixer-upper, be realistic about what repairs/work you can and can't do. It is one thing to replace a door or fix a broken window and quite another to put in wood floors or tear out a wall. If you or someone in your family are a born carpenter and you have an uncle who's a licensed electrician and another who's a plumber, chances are the frustrations of finding help, affording the help, and getting advice are not going to be an issue. However, if you are going into this alone, know your limitations and the costs of hiring a professional if, for some reason, you are unable to do the repairs yourself. Also be aware that some repairs will require a licensed professional.

Another frustration to consider with purchasing a fixer-upper is the quality of living conditions in the home while the repairs are being done. Major projects such as upgrading the kitchen and adding bathrooms can make living conditions very difficult. If your kitchen isn't going to be usable, where are you going to cook? If bathrooms are going to be out of commission for longer than a day, is it reasonable to think you can live in the home? Know what you are up against before you commit yourself.

Q: What are some special concerns I need to consider, or questions I need to ask, before buying a fixer-upper?

A: Below are several concerns and tips consumers looking at fixer-uppers should consider:

■ *Location:* A run-down house in an upscale or even an attractive neighborhood can be a good investment. However, if too many fixer-uppers exist in the area, this may be a sign of a neighborhood where your investment will never be recovered.

■ *Inspections:* Inspections are important in the purchase of every home, but never more so than in the purchase of a fixer-upper. In some ways a home can be compared to a car. A vehicle that shows signs of serious wear and tear on the outside has probably had its engine neglected as well. A home that has gone years with dirty carpet or one that has holes in the walls will probably have had other issues, such as leaky pipes, that have gone uncared for. A lack of maintenance on a home can lead to some serious, costly repairs.

- *Get detailed estimates on repairs:* Don't rely on just assumptions of repair cost. Hire a professional to help calculate the true cost of turning your fixer-upper into your dream home. Renovation isn't cheap.

- *Zoning restrictions:* Look into local zoning restrictions when you find a fixer-upper home that interests you. Be sure you can renovate the home in the way you want. If an area is a designated historic district, you might find regulations and guidelines that you must follow for all the exterior work. Following code restrictions can add costs to the needed repairs.

- *The length of time that will be needed to do repairs:* If you are planning on doing the repairs, how much time will you really be able to devote to the project? If you are having the work contracted, have you asked about the estimated date of completion?

- *Evaluate the floor plan:* A home with good basic layout, even one that is hideously decorated, can be a good fixer-upper. On the flip side, a house that seems a maze of mismatched rooms may have a defective floor plan that no amount of paint and small repairs will remedy.

- *Can you handle the hassles of renovating a home?* It is somewhat jokingly tossed out that renovation is one of the leading causes of divorce. While this may or may not be true, there is no mistaking the fact that fixing up a home can be an emotional strain. Are you up to the added stress? Is your family aware of all that this project will include?

Q: What are the most common defects in an older home?

A: Just because a home is not listed as a fixer-upper, doesn't mean it's free of problems. Older homes are very likely to come with some shortcomings. While most of these defects should be covered in a disclosure, you seldom get the disclosure until you are ready to go to contract. By being observant and becoming a bit of an inspector yourself, you can prevent yourself and your family from falling in love with a home that, in the end, may not meet your expectations.

There are seven common yet major defects to avoid in older homes. All seven could cost a lot of money to correct.

1. **Foundation:** Look for cracked bricks, uneven floors, or doors that won't close. However, not all foundation problems are easy to find. Make sure your inspector is qualified and skilled at finding defects in foundations. If there are foundation problems, be cautious of this purchase because those problems may make the house very hard to sell in the future.

2. **Roof:** Problems with roofs in older homes are very common, and you can and should ask the seller to replace or repair a bad roof. It may be necessary to have this completed before a loan company will make a loan on the property. It can also be an issue for which you can negotiate a lower price.

3. **Heating and cooling systems:** Air conditioners or heating units can also be very costly to repair, and older, poorly functioning systems may result in high energy costs to operate. If the units are very old, there could be potential safety issues such as carbon monoxide

poisoning and fire hazard. Ask about the age of these units, and make sure you have an inspector that is qualified to inspect heating and cooling systems.

4. **Termite damage:** Damage from insects can lead to expensive repairs. If any termite damage is found, it is best to anticipate the worst and do a more in-depth inspection to determine the severity of the problem. You would be wise to ask if the home has been treated annually to protect against these pests. (Some states and lenders require a professional termite inspection report to be made. Make sure your inspector is licensed for this.)

5. **Mold:** In some sections of the country, mold has made some homes uninhabitable. Treatment to stop and kill some forms of mold can be very expensive. You may want to choose another house unless the seller is willing to pay for the removal and repair of all damage. Look around doors and windows for any signs of mold, and if the home reeks of strong air fresheners, ask yourself what odors the owners are trying to conceal.

6. **Electrical wiring:** The electrical wiring and service panel can be a problem in older houses. Depending on the age of the house, there may not be enough current coming into the house for all the modern appliances used today. Different types of wiring are also considered fire hazards and can be very expensive to replace. If this is the situation, have an electrician give you an estimate and use this information to negotiate.

7. **Plumbing:** The plumbing in an older house should be carefully checked. Look for any leaks under toilets, bathtubs, or shower pans. These leaks over time can cause expensive repairs. Look for any discoloring of

the flooring, and in two-story homes, look for discoloration of or repair work in the ceiling. Also make sure the inspector checks out the hot water system.

Q: If I find something wrong with the house, can I ask the sellers to fix it?

A: Yes, you can ask. Wanting repairs made to a home is part of the negotiating process. That doesn't mean the seller will agree to your requests. In a seller's market, when the seller has the upper hand he or she may refuse to negotiate, but you won't know until you ask. All your repair requests should go into the purchase agreement. The request for repairs may slow down the buying process, but don't let your lack of patience stop you from getting a better deal. (See more information about purchase agreements in the "Making an Offer" section.)

Q: What advice is there for homeowners looking to buy a new home?

A: Although buying a new home eliminates some of the worries of discovering age-related problems such as a leaky roof, lead paint, or a faulty water heater, the process of buying a new home isn't totally carefree. Below are common concerns and tips for homebuyers looking at new homes:

Shop for the Builder, Not the Home
While you might like the look of some model homes better than others, you should first consider the builder. Only consider purchasing a home from builders with good

reputations. Even if the home is already completed and looks great, you don't know what kind of construction is behind the walls.

Check Warranties

Don't assume the builder has a warranty; ask to see it and carefully review it before going to contract. In states with strong consumer protection laws, you may be able to take even a nonwarranted builder to court in the case of poor construction. However, do you want to take this chance? Warranties generally come in two types: self-warranted homes and insurance-warranted homes.

1. Self-warranted homes are guaranteed by only the builder. Consumers should be extra careful to note exactly what is and isn't covered, and for how long the coverage stays in effect. Notice the exact language that tells how the builder will correct any problems.

2. Insurance-warranted homes are generally more favored because your property is warranted not only by the builder but also by an insurance company. Normally, the builder still warrants the home, but the insurance backs up the claim, offering you more protection. However, even with the insurance-warranted home, you need to read the details of the warranty to know exactly what is covered.

Neighborhood Concerns

Just because it's a new neighborhood doesn't mean it is going to be a good neighborhood. When purchasing an older home, it's easier to get a sense of what type of neighborhood you are buying into, but it isn't so with new homes in newly developed areas. Make sure you look at the neighborhoods surrounding the area. If too many not-so-nice neighborhoods are nearby, why are you convinced that this new neighborhood will be any different?

Lot Sizes

It's true that you need to be concerned about this in new and old homes. However, it is easier to look at a lot and judge its size if the home is already constructed on the property. Homebuyers looking at empty lots should really take the time to consider how the property will look after the home is constructed. Many of the new developers are using smaller lots and buyers are often surprised at how little yard they are left with after the home is built.

Completion Dates

If you have purchased a not-yet-built home, be prepared for things to take longer than expected. One of the most frequent complaints of those buying a new home is that the move-in date is usually postponed.

Buying the Unknown

Unless you are buying a home that is already constructed, the completed home may not look as you originally expected it to. Many of the model homes come with upgrades, whereas you, in an effort to economize, may have chosen to go with the less-expensive options in flooring, countertops, and fireplaces. While you may know not to expect the upgrades, when you see the home without the niceties of the model home, it may be a disappointment.

Q: How do I find developments during the preconstruction phase?

A: One of the places to find new home developments is in the real estate section of the local paper. In most cities, the Sunday paper has a large section of real estate ads. Look for advertisements with headlines like "Preconstruction Prices." Local real estate agents should also know about new developments.

Q: How can I know if the builder I picked is a good one?

A: You want to pick a builder that has a good history of completing developments. Ask the builder about other developments that he has finished. Drive to them on a weekend, during the day, and take a close look. If you can, ask some of the homeowners how everything went. Discontented homeowners are generally happy to sing about their woes concerning a builder. You shouldn't believe every story you hear, but it should give you cause to further investigate. Also check the builder out with the local Better Business Bureau. You can find your local chapter at *www.bbb.org.*

Q: What should I look for when walking through a newly built house?

A: Basically you should look at all items you would on an older home. Don't let the clean appearance and new smells fool you into believing that a new construction can't have problems. Shoddy construction happens even in the best neighborhoods and high-priced homes. Before you buy, make sure the home is inspected with as much attention to detail as you would exercise in the inspection of an older home. Don't assume a new home is under warranty. Check out all the paperwork before you make a purchase agreement.

Q: What is a punch list?

A: A punch list contains the items the builder must fix before the house can go to closing on a new construction. In most cases, this list is written by you during a walk-through of the house. It should cover anything that has not been completed or is not up to standard. Make sure to check and see if the carpet has been laid correctly and/or that the tile flooring has been lined up straight. Flooring issues seem to be a common problem in new homes.

Q: Are there ways to save on buying a home in a new development?

A: Yes. Besides just looking for the better deals or perhaps the new developments a little farther out of town, there are a number of ways to save when buying a new home. You can buy at the preconstruction stage, which is generally the best pricing on the home. Developers tend to reduce their prices at this stage because they feel nothing brings in customers more than seeing other people buying. This also ensures that you get to pick out all the colors and floor treatments. Of course, the downside is that you will have to wait a long time to get into your new dream home.

Another way to save on a house that is not built is to decline the upgrades. They often do not help increase the value any when you try to resell years later. (Be aware, however, of what it was that attracted you to the model home, so you don't give up one of the upgrades that really made you fall in love with the home.)

Most developers will offer a mortgage package. It may not be a good deal. Be sure to shop around. (Read the "Loan Wisdom" section to learn more about loans.)

The last option is to buy one of the model homes. Builders often discount them just to complete the project so they can move on to their next development. You may get some of the special options or upgrades at no cost, and generally, the yard has been landscaped a lot nicer than you may have opted to pay for. Some developers will even offer the furniture the home has been showcased with as part of the deal. The downside of buying a model home is that you may not get to select any of the wallpaper, paint colors, or floor treatments. The good news is the neighborhood is complete, construction is all done, and you can move in soon.

Q: What is an attached home, and should I consider purchasing one?

A: An attached home is any housing unit that shares a foundation with another home or unit. There are three major types of attached housings:

1. **Condominiums:** A condominium is usually a single apartment where the owner has title to his apartment

unit and shares title to the common areas in the complex.

2. **Townhouses:** Townhouses are usually two-story units that have common walls with other units. The owner has title to the unit and the land under the unit and would share title to any common areas. (There are cases in which townhouses are set up more like cooperatives.)

3. **Cooperatives:** Cooperatives (co-ops) are not a form of architectural design, but of legal ownership. In a co-op, a single unit is owned as shares in a corporation. Owners would have a proprietary lease to live in a certain unit.

Q: Are there special issues I should check out before buying attached housing?

A: Yes. You may need to use a real estate attorney to buy attached housing. The following documents should be carefully reviewed before signing a purchase contract:

- *Master deed:* This is an important document that gives the legal descriptions of all of the property, including the individual units and the common areas.
- *Bylaws:* These are the operating rules for the association. They give the power to the board of directors to assess maintenance fees, write the budget, hire staff, and perform any operating duties.
- *Covenants/conditions:* This document will contain a list of restrictions on the use of the property. Be careful, these restrictions can disallow you to have a cat or a dog in your unit.

■ *Other documents:* You should ask to review the operating budget, current and future assessments, and financial statements of the association.

Q: I have heard of condominiums going bankrupt and of internal conflicts about maintenance and upkeep causing problems for the homeowners; are there warning signs of a problem condominium or cooperative?

A: Yes. Below is a list of things to watch out for.

Too Many of the Units Are Rental Property
One sign that there are problems is when more than 50 percent of the units are rentals. The upkeep of the project may suffer because there tends to be less pride of ownership in the complex.

Low Reserve Funds
A reserve fund is money set aside to take care of improvements and upkeep of the property outside of the individual units. Before purchasing a condo or co-op, you should check out its financial statements, where it should list reserve funds. If the property does not have a healthy reserve fund, you may have to pay a high special assessment to cover any major repairs. This is especially important if the structure is located in a coastal area or an area prone to natural disasters such as floods.

Litigation Problems
If the association is involved in litigation, any funds it has can be sapped, and this can affect resale value.

Contention Between Board Members and Owners

If the members of the board do not get along with each other or the owners, they may make bad decisions that will no doubt affect you and your living conditions.

Q: What is a patio home?

A: Patio homes are normally single-story houses, not attached homes, with a deck or patio area in the rear of the house. These are houses and not apartments. The owners have title to the structure and the land under and around their units. The owner is responsible for the maintenance both inside and outside the home. However, most patio homes come with smaller lots, which require less maintenance than those of regular homes. There will probably be a membership of the owners that will collect maintenance fees covering the maintenance of the entrance to the community and any common areas like tennis courts and pools.

Q: Is a seller-purchased warranty a good benefit?

A: Yes, it can be a good value to select a home in which the seller offers a warranty. But like all things in life, there are warranties and then there are "warranties." Take the time to read and verify just what is covered and how long the coverage lasts.

Another issue to consider is the deductible. This will be the money you will be expected to pay each time you call out a repairman. The industry normally charges between $50 and $100, but it could be as high as $150 for a repairman call. You can see that, if it is a minor problem, it is best to fix it yourself. It is a good idea to contact the Better Business Bureau (BBB) to see if there are any complaints on the warranty company or any of the contractors it uses.

When buying a new home, make sure you get a home warranty. This will protect you in case any problems arise. Remember, a new house has not been tested by time yet. The warranty should protect you from defective materials and poor workmanship. All the appliances will, in most cases, have a one-year warranty, so be sure to get these. The roofing materials, windows, doors, flooring, water heater, and heating and cooling systems will also have warranties. Having this information on hand will spare you the trouble of chasing down information later if you have a problem.

Q: When is it time to make an offer on a property?

A: You have looked at numerous homes and areas until you think you've found the home of your dreams. You have checked out the neighborhood, its schools, and its homeowners association. You've done your homework and know what the community has to offer; you've walked and driven the neighborhood several times, both at night and during different times of the day. You have spoken with neighbors about living in the area. You have checked out the crime rates and the traffic patterns in the area, and you honestly believe this is where you want to live. Okay, maybe you're ready to move to the next step. But before you actually make that offer, read the next chapter to make sure you've got all your ducks in a row.

Part Four

Making an Offer

The search is finished; you've found the house. Now comes the scary part—making the offer. This part of the homebuying process is dreaded only second to getting a loan, and for good reason. You don't want to pay too much, but neither do you want to insult the seller by offering too little—especially when the house is perfect. Well, almost perfect—you want the seller to pay for the new roof and fix the leaky plumbing. And, oh, yeah, the air-conditioning system really needs to be checked out before you sign on the last dotted line.

In this section, you'll find questions covering the information needed to get you through the writing of the purchase agreement. You will learn how to better negotiate a deal and what kinds of inspections are required and who is expected to pay for them. The importance of writing contingencies into your offer is spelled out so you are less likely to make mistakes.

The goal of this chapter is to help you make a good investment, to get the best possible deal, and to prepare you for that final step in the homebuying process—the closing.

Q: I found the house I want to buy; what's my next step?

A: You may think it's time to make the offer, but slow down. You're not quite there yet. Your energy now needs to be spent on looking seriously at how much you are willing to pay for this property and how much the property is worth.

If you have been looking at homes for a while, you should have a pretty good idea of what similar houses are listed for. But let's not take things for granted. Just to be sure, ask your agent to let you see the selling prices of similar homes, going back at least a year. Pick out all sales for houses similar to the home you're interested in—try to get as close a match as possible (same number of bedrooms, bathrooms, pool, amenities). In an active market you'll find half a dozen sales or more.

Extra features such as a new kitchen, bathroom, or other remodeling do add to the value of a house. However, they do not normally make the house significantly more valuable than its neighbors. Any house that is priced more than 5 percent above its neighbors because of improvements may be overpriced. It's important not to feel sorry for sellers who dropped a lot of money into remodeling and are now trying to get every penny back from you. Homeowners are constantly being warned to do remodeling projects only for their own enjoyment and to never expect to get the money back when selling.

Another thing you must do before you make your offer is go through the house one more time. This time, be prepared to do your own inspection. Bring a pen and paper and take notes so you won't forget things. Really look at the condition of the house. Are there things that you want to be fixed before you move in? Now ask yourself if you're willing to pay for those repairs. If not, these are things you need to make clear in your offer.

Also, take a close look at the items you believe come with the home. Is the cabinet flanking the wall a built-in or is it removable and the sellers plan to take it with them? Does the beautiful chandelier hanging over the dining room table come with the home, or is it the seller's family heirloom and they don't plan on leaving it. You might be surprised to learn of all the items that past homebuyers thought came with a home, only to discover too late that they were wrong. Know what you are paying for; if unsure, ask.

Q: Should I ask my agent what to offer for the house?

A: While it seems like the most logical approach, asking your agent isn't the best idea. Most agents would prefer an easy negotiation, meaning you should make an offer the seller can't refuse. While your objective isn't to be refused, neither is it to give the seller the better deal. Remember, unless you've hired a buyer's broker, the agent isn't working for you. In many ways asking your agent how much to offer is similar to asking a used-car salesperson how much you should offer to pay for the car. An agent's commission is dependent on the price of the home, the more you pay for the property, the higher their commission. So, basically, you are asking the wrong person.

Q: Should I have my own appraisal done so I will be sure that I'm not offering too much?

A: This is an option. However, it is a $300 to $400 option. Most people find they can do a fair estimate with the list of sales in the area. However, if, for some reason, you feel unsure, calling in an appraiser may give you peace of mind and could prevent you from paying too much.

The appraisal is generally done by the lender to make sure the property is worth the amount of the loan. In most instances you will be paying for that service, but a prior appraisal may not be accepted by the lender.

Q: I've heard it is reasonable to offer 10 percent less than the asking price—is this true?

A: This is another question that is hard to answer because it varies from situation to situation. In a seller's market, when there are fewer houses available, the seller might not be willing to come down on the price at all. If you go in with a low bid, and another offer comes through for the asking price, you could lose the house. In a true buyer's market, you may find sellers so eager to sell that they'll come down as much as 20 percent. Then there are homes that are amazingly overpriced and it would be foolish to follow the 10 percent "rule." The best piece of advice is to use your judgment. If it's a seller's market, accept that you may be paying more; if it's a buyer's market, the seller may be the one to give a little. The idea here is to get fair market price.

That said, let's look at the common scenario, when the market is fairly even. Sellers in most markets ask more than they are willing to take for their homes. They list the house at an above-market price and expect the homebuyer to negotiate. So if you pay what the seller is asking, you could be paying too much. The trick is figuring out how much less a seller will take.

Unless you can read minds, you do not know. That means you have to learn through the negotiating process. Your offer and each counteroffer the seller brings to the table will give you insight to his true asking price and where he will draw the line.

Q: Can I negotiate the price of a new home?

A: Yes. To many consumers, this comes as a surprise because the deal seems so cut and dried—they will build you this house, with these amenities, for this price, end of story. However, just as you can and should negotiate for a resale home, you should feel free to negotiate when purchasing a new home.

Even if your builder does not have the flexibility to work with the actual price, he may be able to work with you on the upgrades.

Q: Exactly what is a purchase agreement?

A: Sometimes called the "sales offer," this is the key document that will decide how the rest of the sale is to be handled. Everything from how much you pay, when you pay, what repairs will be done by the owner, inspection dates, and home warranties is dependent on what is written in this important document. Also included are any other disclosures, the time the seller has to respond to the offer, and the move-in date.

When you are ready to make that offer, tell your agent or lawyer. They will have the document ready and a pen handy. But remember, take your time and be sure to state all of your conditions. If you want the seller to pay for those leaky pipes, it needs to be written into the purchase agreement. You can't suddenly remember something you wanted to add and request to make another purchase agreement.

Q: What are contingencies and how do they protect me?

A: Contingencies are the conditions you list in your purchase agreement. Basically, a contingency is saying, "I will buy the home if. . . ." It is up to you to tell your agent or lawyer your conditions. Most of the common contingencies such as roof repair or leaky pipes are already written into purchasing agreements and need only to be checked. Others will need to be written in. Below are some common contingencies:

Mortgage Contingency Clause
If, for some reason, your loan falls through or the interest rates are increased, you need to be legally released from the contract to purchase the home. Make sure you write in the purchase agreement that your sale is contingent on loan approval.

Termite Inspection
In some parts of the country, especially with attached housing, a "termite bond" must be shown at the closing.

Home Inspection Contingency
Make sure it states in your contract that the sale is contingent on the assumption that the plumbing, heating/cooling, electrical system, and appliances are all found to be in working order. While you can request that the seller pay for the inspection, most homebuyers prefer to pay for the inspector to make sure he is working for them and not the seller.

Move-in Date

You probably want to move into the house right after the closing; however, problems could arise with the sellers and they may request a few more days or weeks. Most times, a homebuyer will put in a clause that the seller must pay rent.

Sale of an Existing Home

If you are also selling another home and can only buy the new home if the old one is sold, make sure this is included in the document.

The Promise of a Clear Title

You will want a clause in the contract stating that the sellers must provide a clear title—meaning no tax or other liens against the property.

A Definition of Personal Property

While this may seem odd, some sellers think nothing of pulling out a built-in cabinet that you assumed came with the home.

Sale Is Subject to Buyer's Review of Community Regulations

This means you don't find any surprises in the community's covenants. Hopefully, you have already reviewed the restrictions with the homeowners association.

Closing Day Inspection

A good contract will give the buyer the right to inspect the property on the day of closing before the meeting takes place. This is your last chance to make sure all your conditions have been met.

Closing Costs

This is another item that is negotiable. Let's say you don't think the seller will agree to the price you want, but you may be able to convince him to pay for some of the closing costs.

Liability and Maintenance

This means that the seller agrees to hand over the house to you in the same condition it was when you signed the contract.

Subject to Review by Buyer's Attorney

If you are using an attorney, you may want to give your attorney the right to review the property.

Any Other Contingencies That You Want Met Before the Sale Is Final

Remember this is your last chance at getting what you want. Make sure the conditions are clear.

Q: Can I have too many contingencies?

A: This is another question where the answer may vary depending on the market and the personality of the seller. In a seller's market, when it is likely the owner will receive more than one offer, he will in all likelihood go with the offer that has fewer contingencies. A purchasing agreement with fewer contingencies generally means a better chance that the deal will actually go through. And, in most cases, it means the seller will have fewer hassles and fewer financial concerns.

Even when the market is average, it is wise to be reasonable. Attempt to put yourself in the seller's place. If your offer is filled with too many contingencies, he or she may feel you are attempting to take advantage of the situation and may very well turn it down.

Then again, if you really feel the house is not a good deal without the seller's agreement to make or pay for the repairs, then stick to your guns.

Q: What are some tips for negotiating?

A: While there are lots of people who are born negotiators, people who live to haggle over price, there are more of us who shy away from the whole negotiation process. However, brushing up on a few negotiation skills can help the non-negotiating type be more assertive and will even give an edge to the best of hagglers.

Don't Be Insulting
When money is concerned, it is sometimes easy to speak our minds before we weigh our words. It is best to remember that this is business and your personal feelings should be kept in check. If you insult an agent or seller, a business transaction can turn into a personal fight, which you may very well lose.

Be Determined and Don't Show Your Cards
It isn't wise to let your agent know exactly how high you will go to get the house. He or she may express this to the seller, or the seller's agent, and then you will end up paying the top price, not knowing the seller would have taken less. On the flip side, if you convince your agent you won't pay any more than is listed in your counteroffer or that you expect the seller to agree to all your contingencies, the agent may express this to the seller and you may get what you want.

Use Time on Your Side

By limiting the amount of time the seller can have before answering your offer (twelve to twenty-four hours is average), you force the seller to come to a decision, which may prevent a better offer from being placed on the table.

Don't Forget to Compromise

If the seller's counteroffer is very close to what you asked for, you should be reasonable.

Don't Get Hung up on Only the Price

Some sellers can be adamant about getting their asking price. If you give them their price, they may be willing to give in in other areas, perhaps personal property or early possession, and they may even be more likely to pay some of the closing costs.

Q: What happens when the seller counteroffers?

A: This shouldn't worry you. This means the seller is willing to negotiate. What you need to do is read over his counter-offer. Give it serious consideration and decide if his offer is fair, or if you should counteroffer yourself. Your agent will probably write in your counteroffer and send it back to the seller. This process can go back and forth between seller and buyer numerous times.

Q: What happens if we can't reach an agreement?

A: Unfortunately, you must be willing to walk away or pay the seller's price. However, if you have countered several times and are not making headway, make sure the seller knows that you are considering walking. It might be wise to have your agent draft a letter with the counteroffer and state that this is your final offer. The seller may rethink his position, or you may simply have to walk away. Only you can decide how much is too much to pay for a house you really want.

Q: What is earnest money?

A: As soon as you have filled out the purchase agreement, you will be expected to give a deposit. This deposit is often referred to as earnest money. It is money you put down to demonstrate that you are serious about buying the house. It can be in the form of a personal check, a certified check, or a money order.

It isn't wise to give the check to the seller. As a matter of fact, the check should be made out to the broker on record. Also add the word *trustee* or *fiduciary agent* after the name of the broker. This will protect your money because the check will be deposited only as money held in trust. If your offer is accepted, the earnest money becomes part of your down payment or closing costs.

Q: How much earnest money should I set aside and what happens to it if the deal falls through?

A: Though the amount of earnest money can vary with local customs and conditions, the amount must be substantial enough to demonstrate good faith. The amount usually falls between 1 and 5 percent of the purchase price. However, in some states, $500 to $1,000 is considered sufficient.

The real estate laws in all states require that your earnest money be returned to you if the offer is not accepted by the seller or if the contingencies agreed on in the contract are not met by the seller. If the money has been deposited, it may take some time to get the money returned. Generally, the real estate agent keeps the check clipped to the contract and will just hand the check back over to you. However, if you back out of the deal without valid reasons, or for those that are not covered in the contract, you may have to forfeit the entire amount.

Q: When is the right time to start shopping for insurance?

A: The time to start shopping for insurance is right after you have signed the purchase contract on a property. Lenders will require that you have a hazard insurance policy that will pay the lender in case there is damage to the house from fire, smoke, wind, or hail. You will need certain information on the property and yourself. You will need the address of the house, the location of fire stations and fire plugs, your present address, and your Social Security number. Be sure to let the insurance company know about outbuildings such as a garage or a garden shed, and tell them if there is a pool.

Also, your lender will require you to have flood insurance if the property is found to be in a flood-prone area. Your standard hazard insurance will protect you in the event of water damage due to a broken pipe or a running toilet. Flood insurance covers you in the event that your home sustains damage from rising water. Flood insurance can be obtained through the federal government under the National Flood Insurance Program. You can get more information on the Web at *www.fema.gov*. This coverage can also be bought at most insurance offices. An average cost for an annual policy is between $150 and $200 for $85,000 of coverage.

In some parts of the country, there are additional hazards that need special coverage. In California, special earthquake coverage is a good idea. In Florida and other coastal areas, it may be a good idea to look at additional windstorm coverage for damage caused by hurricanes.

Q: What other types of insurance should I consider?

A: Besides the insurance that the lenders require and the special hazard coverages, there are others you may want to consider. With the purchase of a house being possibly the largest investment you will make in a lifetime, you will probably want to protect this investment.

The most common insurance to consider is a homeowner's policy. It will cover loss of your personal possessions and will protect you from liability if someone is hurt on the property.

If you have an extensive jewelry collection or other types of valuables, you may want to look at buying a personal "floater." A standard homeowner's policy has limits on what it will pay out for such items. So, first check your standard homeowner's policy and look at its limits of coverage. Then request a quote on a personal articles floater.

Q: How do I get the best price for the insurance I need for the new house?

A: One of the best ways to lower your insurance cost is to have a high deductible on all policies. Insurance is meant to protect you in the event of catastrophes, not small claims that you can fix yourself or easily pay to have repaired.

Also, look at the value the insurance adjusters place on your house. If they inflate the price, you will be paying more. This is also true if you have homeowner's insurance and they inflate the value of the contents of your house.

It is also good to make sure that you are insuring only the home and not the land it is on. For example, if you pay $100,000 for a home, the land may be worth as much as $20,000. You should carry insurance for only $80,000, or for the value of the home.

Some insurance policies allow you a deduction for adding a home security system, dead bolt locks, or smoke alarms. If you are planning to install these items, contact your potential insurance agent to find out what types of devices they require to reduce your rates. If you have been with the same insurance company for a number of years, you may also get a discount on a new homeowner's policy. It is also very helpful if you have been claim-free during this time.

For first-time buyers, it might be wise to get a quote from the company that you have your automobile coverage with. Because you are already a client, they may give you a reduction on your house premiums and on your auto rates.

To keep everyone honest, it is best to get at least four quotes on your home insurance. Be sure when you are comparing policies, that you check not only the costs, but also the amount and type of coverage.

Q: Do I need insurance for a condo or co-op?

A: Yes. It is a good idea to have coverage. There are special policies for attached types of living quarters. Part of your monthly maintenance fee pays for hazard insurance and liability coverage for the common areas, which the owners association or cooperative board will have purchased for the entire complex. However, this coverage will not help you in your own unit if there is a burst pipe or smoke damage. It is also a good idea to get homeowner's coverage to protect your personal belongings and help with liability if someone is hurt in your unit and sues.

Q: Who pays for the inspection, how much does it cost, and how long does it take?

A: Generally, the buyer pays for the inspection. In some cases, the buyer may request that the seller pay for the inspection, but it's not really a good idea. The buyer is the one who will benefit from the information from the inspection, so you need to know that the inspector has only your interest in mind. If the inspector is being paid by the seller, his loyalties may lean toward the seller. As recommended in the "Shopping for a Home" section, it is best for you to be on the lookout for major problems before you put together a formal written offer. This way, if there are any glaring defects, you will not waste any time or money on hiring an inspector.

The inspection should take two to three hours to complete, depending on the size of the house, its age, its type, and the part of the country it is in. An inspection should cost from $200 to $500. It is important to ask the inspector if there are additional charges for going on the roof and crawling under the house. This is the best way to determine the condition of the roof and get a better understanding of the soundness of the foundation and plumbing.

Also ask what the charges are for inspection for radon gas and, if there is a well, for water testing. Depending on the age of the structure, you may have to request the cost of inspection for asbestos and lead paint. And depending on the location of the property, you may have to pay extra for an inspection for termites or other pests.

The inspector may not be licensed for this type of inspection and may have to refer you to some other company. Be sure to verify what these charges will be. You do not want any money surprises during a homebuying process.

Q: When should the inspection take place?

A: The inspection should take place only after you have made an offer, the offer has been accepted, and all parties have signed the purchase agreement. Be sure that the sales contract has a contingency that allows you to back out if the inspection shows any major problems. Remember it is rare for buyers to have to pay for inspections on more than one property during the entire house-hunting process.

Before you hire the inspector, make sure you or your agent schedules this with the sellers, who are probably still living in the home. In addition to setting up the time and date for the inspection, you should also get the seller's full disclosure on the property. This should be a written document, not just a verbal list. Give a copy of the disclosure to the house inspector. The inspector can then take a closer look at potential problems. With this information, the inspector can also verify how bad the disclosed problems are and give an estimate of what they will cost to repair.

Q: What are the inspector's responsibilities, and what should I know before hiring one?

A: The inspector will not determine if the price of the house is a good value. He will determine if the house will be a safe place to live, and he can give you an estimated cost for the repairs that may be needed.

You will want the inspector to check the plumbing; water heater; waste disposal; electrical system; heating, ventilation, and air-conditioning systems (HVAC); foundation; doors; windows; walls; floors; ceilings; roof; and the possible presence of pests such as termites. In some states, the lender may require that an inspection be done for termites. Be sure the inspector is qualified to do all inspections needed for the purchase of the home.

A very wise thing to do is to take the time to be with the inspector throughout the examination of the property. If any problems are found, you can get answers to any questions you have right away, and you will have a better understanding of the problem. The inspector also may be able to provide you with estimates on what the repairs would cost. With this information, you will know how to negotiate with the seller on the price of the property. Also, during the examination, you can learn more about the maintenance and preservation of the house.

Another thing you need to know is that, if the home inspector finds any potentially serious problems, a special inspector should be called in to make a final determination. This could include professionals who specialize in recognizing and repairing electrical, plumbing, heating and cooling, or structural problems. There are also health-related inspections you may want to complete. These include tests for radon gas, asbestos, lead, or problems with the water supply.

Q: What is the best way to find a home inspector and how do I know if he is reliable?

A: As in most things, the best way to find a good inspector is through a personal recommendation from someone you trust. You want an inspector who will be thorough and tough, not a person who will overlook small issues. If you do not have contacts, home inspectors can be found in the Yellow Pages under either "Building Inspection Service" or "Home Inspection Service." You could also go on the Web to *www.ashi.com*. This site will provide a list of inspectors in your area who are members of the American Society of Home Inspectors (ASHI).

Making sure your inspector belongs to the ASHI is one way to be sure he or she is qualified for the job. You can also check with the Better Business Bureau. You can find your local chapter in the Business White Pages, or look them up on the Web at *www.bbb.org* to find out how to contact your local branch.

Q: Can a house fail inspection?

A: No. A home inspection will not pass or fail a property. It will review the condition of the house and indicate what needs to be repaired or replaced. It may also give you an estimate of what the repairs will cost. Then it is up to you to decide if the home is worth buying at the offer you listed in the purchase agreement.

Don't be surprised or alarmed when the inspector hands over the report with his findings. Some homebuyers expect a home to be perfect and homes seldom are. Almost all homes will have several things that need to be repaired. Some of the more common finds include an aged or inadequate water heater, nonworking appliances such as dishwashers and built-in ranges and ovens, leaky faucets, hairline settling cracks in the foundation (these will be listed as hairline cracks, not a cracked foundation), and the normal dirt and grime. These items are very easily fixed and should not delay closing.

Other items that may prove to be more worrisome and costly to repair are peeling or bubbling exterior paint; a bad roof; deteriorating gutters; leaks in the roof at the flashings; excessive moisture in the attic; pests such as termites, bats, mice, or squirrels; inadequate insulation; plumbing problems; and window repair. If the inspector finds one of the above defects, it doesn't necessarily mean you should walk away, but it would be wise to go back to the table and talk money.

There are also several defects that, if found in a home, should make you seriously consider walking away from the deal. If you have done as recommended and put an inspection contingency clause in the contract, you should be released from the deal with no problem, and your earnest money should be refunded. These defects are unsafe or inadequate drinking water, a nonfunctioning or malfunctioning private sewer system (septic tank or cesspool), uncontrollable basement water problems, uneven settling or a buckling foundation, and location in a floodplain. (If the property is on low land or near a river or stream, investigate. The U.S. Geological Survey has mapped most floodplain areas in this country. Federal flood insurance is available to residents of floodplain areas. Most lenders will not write a mortgage without it.)

Q: Should I have a new home inspected?

A: While it may not always be a requirement for new homes, it is a very good idea. Remember, just because a home is new doesn't mean it's good. Just because it is shiny and clean doesn't mean that there isn't some very poor construction work holding it up. If you are having the home built, you may want to have it inspected several times during the construction phase as well. A good builder should never discourage inspections.

Q: What can I do if the builder hasn't completed some of the smaller items in my home?

A: The best way to get the builder to complete all items on the punch list is to delay the closing. This will get his attention fast. Most builders need the money from each completed house as soon as possible to help their cash flow.

Many builders will promise to come and do the remaining minor repairs after closing, but this is not always recommended. Do you want strangers coming into your home? Do you want the inconvenience of having to work within their schedules? In addition, if something ends up falling short of your standards, you have lost the leverage you had in refusing to close the deal until after the problem has been corrected.

Q: Can I count on moving into my newly built house when the builder says I can?

A: While some builders seem to make promises they know they can't keep just to get you to buy, others have good intentions. However, even the best builders cannot predict some problems that may arise and delay the completion of the house. There will always be some uncertainty about when the house will actually be ready. There can be weather delays, construction snags, and material delays. You may not have the luxury of time to wait for the house. If this is the case, consider buying a preconstructed home.

One thing new homeowners need to be leery of is if the builder offers a cash allowance in lieu of completing all the items on the punch list. The builder knows what it will cost to fix all the items, and in most cases, his reason for offering the cash is to save himself the worry and expense.

Q: What are building codes and what happens if a violation is uncovered during the inspection?

A: Building codes are state or locally adopted regulations, enforceable by law, that control the design, construction, repair, and use and occupancy of a structure, as well as the quality of building materials used to build it.

It is important to know that sellers may not be required to bring an older home up to the latest codes. In most areas of the country, there are grandfather clauses. This means the property owner does not have to update the property to meet new codes that were adopted after the house was built. After the seller becomes aware of these building code violations, he or she is required to add these to any disclosures. As the buyer, it is a good idea to add this issue as a contingency in the purchase contract. Sometimes it is messy and costly to bring a structure up to the latest building codes. Before you agree to buy a property that does not meet the codes, get an estimate. You may feel you no longer want to buy the house.

Q: What is an appraisal?

A: As a potential homeowner, there are two types of appraisals you should know about. Your lender will require the home you've selected to be appraised. It wants to be sure the property is worth what it will loan you. You will be paying for this service at closing. It typically runs from $200 to $400, depending on the size, value, and location of the property. However, in some cases, if you choose an approved appraiser recommended by the lender, you may not have to pay for the required appraisal.

The second type of appraisal that will affect you as a homeowner is the appraisal that the taxing authority does to set your property taxes. This type of appraisal is used to place a value on your property, and you will then be taxed based on this amount.

One thing that is often misunderstood about appraisals is how the appraised value differs from the market value. Appraised value is what price the house will actually bring at a given point in time. Market value is quoted by a real estate agent or broker who offers an informal estimate of market value based on sales of nearby properties.

Q: What happens during an appraisal?

A: The appraiser will inspect the house to check its condition and count the number and types of rooms. They will measure the sizes of the rooms and draw up the floor plan. They will review the site plan to make sure it agrees with the property as it is the day of the appraisal. Pictures will be taken for the report. The information gathered from the site will be compared with at least three other similar homes that are in the area and have been sold in the past six months.

Q: What happens if the house doesn't appraise for the requested selling price?

A: The lender may back out of the loan if the appraisal doesn't meet up to the loan amount. If you put a contingency clause regarding loan approval in the purchasing agreement, you are not required to go ahead with the deal. However, if you really want the house, there are several things you might try.

First, go to the seller and see if he will come down on the price. If that isn't an option, you can attempt to boost a low appraisal. Start by getting your hands on a copy of the report. If the appraiser has overlooked a valuable feature of the home or neglected to consider a recent "higher" comparable sale, take your complaint to the loan representative. If you simply believe the appraiser did a poor job, you may request to have a new report done by another appraiser. One last thing you may do is offer to increase your down payment. This may persuade the lender to overlook the low appraisal.

Part Five

Closing and Contract Facts

It is finally here. You are about to become owners of the home you selected, the home you've dreamed about, scrutinized, described to countless friends and family members, and mentally decorated. Hopefully, you have arrived at this important day without too many stress-induced headaches. And while this is definitely a time to celebrate, it is not the time to go on a mental vacation. Some people believe the closing to be just the signing of a few papers, but in truth, there is a lot happening at the closing and it needs your full attention. You are about to make the biggest, or one of the biggest, purchases in your life. The realization can be both exciting and nerve-wracking. But take a deep breath—the whole process is coming to a close, the deal is almost done, you have never been closer to owning the home as you are right now.

In this section, we will cover questions regarding what you will need to bring with you to the closing, what you can expect to happen, and what you should be watching out for. The goal of this section is to make sure the last step of buying a home goes smoothly and is trouble-free. It is to prevent you from getting charged twice for the same service and, ultimately, to set you on the course to being a responsible homeowner.

Q: What exactly is a closing and what makes up closing costs?

A: The closing is the meeting of all concerned parties in order to transfer the title of the property. It is during this event that everything finally becomes official. You become a homeowner and the seller gets his money.

Closing costs generally equal 2 to 7 percent of your home's sale price. Usually, you have to pay these costs in cash, in addition to the money you've earmarked for a down payment. The different fees that make up closing costs can vary from lender to lender and from state to state. In general, closing costs are made up of the following:

- Attorney's or escrow fees (yours and, in some cases, those of your lender)
- Property taxes (to cover tax period to date)
- Loan origination fee (this also may cover lender's administrative cost)
- Interest (paid from date of closing to 30 days before first monthly payment)
- Recording fees
- Survey fee
- First premium of mortgage insurance (when applicable)
- Loan discount points
- Title insurance (both yours and the lender's)
- Paid receipt for homeowner's insurance policy (fire and flood insurance if applicable)
- First payment to escrow account for future real estate taxes and insurance
- Any documentation fees

Q: Are there fees I should question?

A: You should look at every fee before signing on the dotted line. However, there are common areas that may need to be reviewed more carefully. Many of these fees, those that are lender related, should be questioned at the time of loan approval and rechecked during the actual closing.

- **Loan fees:** A loan fee is a charge that is tacked on in addition to your points. A lender may state that the fee is covering the documentation work of funding the money. A good lender will charge only a small loan fee or no fee at all.
- **Account setup fees:** An account fee is basically charging you to set up the account and for the payment book or monthly invoices. It is wise to question these charges.
- **Document preparation fees:** Look at what they are charging you. Some lenders charge extreme amounts for simply hitting a few keys on the keyboard. Question the lender about these fees. You might be surprised what a simple question may get you.
- **Recording fees:** It is normal for the escrow company to charge fees for recording documents; however, it is not too uncommon to find one and sometimes more duplicate charges tacked onto the bill.
- **Any charges that leave you asking, "What's this?":** It is an unfortunate fact that some lenders employ creative, and sometimes illegal, ways to tack on dubious charges.

Q: Can I get the seller to pay some of my closing costs?

A: By negotiating up front, you may be able to get the seller to pay some of the closing costs. You should have your agent or lawyer write up a contingency clause in the purchase agreement detailing exactly what fees you want the seller to fund. Your success in getting the seller to agree to these conditions is dependent on several variables. One variable is the seller's overall willingness to negotiate. The other factor is connected to the overall real estate market at the time of purchase. If it is a seller's market, most sellers will outright refuse to pay for any of the closing costs and may not even budge on the asking price.

Q: What is a "HUD/1" or settlement statement, and why is it considered one of the most important documents to review during closing?

A: This is the document that itemizes services provided to you and the fees each service costs. It should be filled out by the closing agent and must be given to you at or before the closing. You should refer to this document to make sure you are not being charged twice for the same service. If it is given to you in advance of the closing, study it carefully and take it with you to the closing; if you are given it at the closing, take the time to go over it and check and double-check any fees against this document.

Real estate agents and real estate brokers have said they are constantly seeing duplicate fees, and sometimes just bogus fees, being tacked onto the buyer's to-be-paid list. In some of these instances, the professional person worked for the seller and therefore could not speak up on behalf of the buyer. These professionals tell us that most of these charges should have been deleted and would have been if the homeowner had gone over the HUD/1 statement carefully.

Q: I've heard of no-cost mortgages where there are no closing costs; do they exist?

A: Yes. Some lenders do offer no-cost mortgages. But don't be fooled—there are costs involved. What the lender is doing is rolling the closing costs into the mortgage. While this may be a good option for those who are short on up-front cash, it comes with a downside. Either you will be paying higher interest rates or you will be taking out a bigger loan, and both of these generally lead to higher monthly payments. (See the "Loan Wisdom" section for more information on loans.)

Another thing to be aware of with these no-cost mortgages is that you will still be expected to pay for certain items such as hazard insurance. Make sure all the details are clear before you commit yourself.

Q: Are closing costs negotiable?

A: Most are, but some aren't. Lots of people assume everything is negotiable in the homebuying process. While this is not 100 percent true, it is true that the people who are willing to ask about negotiations are generally the consumers who end up getting a better deal. So, by all means, it doesn't hurt to ask. However, the right time to ask about closing costs connected with the lender is when you get the loan, not on closing day.

That said, there are some costs involved in the closing that are set fees. To get this information, ask the prospective lenders during the interview process about what is and isn't negotiable. If one lender offers a better deal, tell the others. A little competition will usually get them in a better negotiating mood.

Q: Are there ways to save on my closing costs?

A: Yes. One way to save on closing costs is to shop for a loan that has fewer fees. Be aware that fewer fees generally means higher rates. It is up to you to do your homework and see which option is best for you. Another way to save on closing costs is to look at the fees that you will be required to pay (hazard insurance, appraisals, and inspections) and shop around for the best deal. Many lenders and agents will give you referrals. Don't just take one name and run with it. Call and get estimates, and make your decision on the best deal offered by the most dependable company. Some lenders may not charge you for the appraisal if you use their recommended appraiser. Ask if this is the case. One more small way to cut closing costs is to schedule the closing at the end of the month so you pay less in prepaid interest.

Q: Where does the closing take place?

A: The answer to this question varies from state to state. In some regions of the country, notably in the Northeast, the closing might be held at a lawyer's office. In contrast, the scene of a settlement on the West Coast might be the office of an escrow agent. In other places, you might find the closing process taking place at the lending institution, a title insurance company, or a real estate office.

Q: What can I expect to happen on closing day?

A: Because each state has it own closing scenarios and local customs, it is best to ask your real estate agent or lawyer what you can expect to have happen during the closing. That said, there are some general guidelines that you may find in most closing customs.

You will probably present your paid homeowner's insurance policy or a binder and receipt showing that the premium has been paid. The closing agent is likely to list the money you owe the seller (the remainder of the down payment, prepaid taxes, etc.) and then the money the seller owes you (unpaid taxes; prepaid rent, if applicable). The seller will then be required to provide proof of any inspection, warranties, and so forth.

All questions about money owed, warranties, and inspections will be answered, and then you'll be expected to sign the mortgage papers, promising to repay the loan, and another document explaining the rights of the lender if you default on the loan. The seller will then hand over the title to the house in the form of a signed deed.

You will have to pay the lender's agent all closing costs, and in return, he will give you a settlement statement of all items for which you have paid. The deed and mortgage will then be recorded in the state Registry of Deeds, and you will be a homeowner.

Q: What should I do before closing?

A: You need to either hire a moving service or enlist the help of friends and family to help you move the heavier furniture and appliances. If you are going with a moving service, make sure you allow plenty of time to schedule this event. Also explain that you are waiting for the closing of the home, which means the move-in day could be delayed. It is best to use a moving company that is recommended to you, and always check with the Better Business Bureau to ensure that the company provides the quality of service it promises.

At least two weeks prior to your closing day, it is recommended that you call and arrange for your utilities (phone, electricity, gas, trash disposal, cable, and any other utilities you may have) to be turned on or to be transferred into your name. Give them a tentative move-in date.

Hopefully, you have arranged to do one last walkthrough of the property—generally, this is done on the same day as the closing. This is your last chance to notice things that have not been fixed or finished, to make sure all the property that you assumed came with the home is still intact, and to make sure there hasn't been any damage to the home since the home was inspected.

Q: What do I do if I find some of the contingencies in my purchasing agreement have not been met?

A: If something is not acceptable, do not sign the closing documents. Even a promise from the seller that he or she will correct the problem isn't sufficient. If you do sign the agreement, you may have to take the seller to court if, for some reason, he or she later refuses to make good on his or her promises.

When the property is a new home, many sellers are quick to state that the items are all under warranty and therefore you can close without concern. Be aware, however, that you will probably be at their mercy and have to work with their schedule to make the repairs and to complete the work. While it is not uncommon for builders to do minor repairs or jobs after the closing, it can be a stressful and frustrating experience, taking away from the pleasure of getting established in your new home.

Q: How do I handle a late closing?

A: While this is a big disappointment, it is not uncommon. Because there are so many things contingent on the closing—a clear title, repair work that needs to be completed by contractors, and all the paperwork being properly filed—chances are, something may very well delay the process a few days or even a few weeks.

Because the closing is likely to be postponed, it is important that you do not make any unbreakable commitments that depend on that particular date. Inform the moving company and utilities companies that the move-in date is dependent on the closing of a home. In most cases, movers and utility companies know that this means the date could be changed. If you are renting, tell your landlord of the situation and ask in advance what would happen if a problem arises. Would you be able to stay a little longer? Some landlords are understanding and will allow you to pay by the week; others may expect you to pay a full month's rent. Whatever the case, know this up front so you won't be hit by some unexpected problems or money issues.

Q: What will I need to bring to the closing?

A: Your agent or lawyer should provide you with a list of what you will need to bring to the closing; however, below is a general list:

1. **Money:** Before you attend the closing, be sure to purchase a certified check for the predetermined amount, which should have been told to you by the agent. It is

also important that you have some money in a checking account for unexpected expenses.

2. **Personal identification:** You probably have this with you at all times, but you may be asked to show proof that you are who you say you are. A driver's license, a passport, or a birth certificate will suffice.

3. **A file with all important documents pertaining to your home:** Included in this file should be a copy of your loan commitment letter, the contract to purchase, a copy of your homeowner's insurance policy, as well as any hazard insurance—showing you at least made the first quarter's premium payment. Also included in the file should be the lender's statement of settlement charges and the HUD/1 form if given to you earlier.

4. **Your wits and your patience:** Even with the assurance of your agent or lawyer that he or she will be in charge, you need to be aware of what you are signing and be careful that you are not being charged twice for the same service.

Q: What can I expect to get at the closing?

A: It will seem like an endless amount of paperwork, some of which will require your signature, and some of which is just for you to take home to read. Below is a list of things you might expect to walk away with at the end of this all-important meeting:

■ Settlement statement, HUD/1 form (In some instances, this document is given to you in advance.)
■ Truth-in-lending statement
■ Mortgage note

- Mortgage or deed of trust
- Binding sales contract (This should be prepared by the seller; your lawyer or broker should review it.)
- Keys to your new home

Q: Who needs to be at the closing?

A: This varies from state to state. In some states, it is a full house, with the seller, his lawyer, the selling and listing agent/broker, the buyer and buyer's lawyer, and the representative of the title company. In contrast, in other states, it can be just the buyer and the escrow agent.

Q: Can I move into the new house before closing?

A: This can be negotiated with the seller. The seller, with the help of his or her real estate agent, may require that you sign a rental agreement. It may sound funny to have to sign a rental agreement on a house you will own, but understand that, until the closing is finished, the house still belongs to the seller and this is his way of protecting himself if the sale falls through.

Q: What if the seller does not want to move until after the closing?

A: This is not unusual, but it can be a problem for you. Many times a seller is waiting for another house to become available. If something happens to delay his or her move-in date, he or she may very well ask to either move the closing back or to make other arrangements. Waiting another couple of weeks, or even months, can be difficult for an excited homebuyer; even so, the situation does happen and needs to be considered.

While you may be able to postpone the closing, you also could consider having a rental agreement written up that offers to allow the seller to remain living in the house for a designated period of time—at a set charge. However, this option is better discussed earlier so no one is left scrambling around in a panic to make sudden changes. Normally, this is a subject that is discussed at the time the purchasing agreement is drawn up. (You can read more about the purchase contract on page 138.)

Q: What is a title search and who pays for it?

A: A title search is a professional examination of public records to determine the ownership of a piece of property. They look for any liens on a property, such as mortgages, encumbrances, taxes due, or restrictions that might affect the title from being free and clear. If liens are found, the seller can pay to clear them, or in some cases, the buyer can take care of them.

Depending on the custom in the area, the title search can be paid by either the seller or the buyer. However, this is negotiable and should have been covered in the purchase agreement.

Q: What is title insurance?

A: This is a policy that protects against any defects in the title that may have been overlooked during the title search. For example, a contractor who worked on the house may not have been paid for his work and then places a lien on the house.

Q: Are there other terms that I might need to know to get me through the closing process?

A: Below is a list of some of the common terms you may hear at the closing:

Abstract of Title: This is a synopsis of the property's history written by the title company or sometimes a lawyer. This document will include past changes in ownership, liens, mortgages, charges, encumbrances, or encroachments.

Acceleration Clause: This is a stipulation in a mortgage agreement that allows the lender to demand full payment of the loan if the scheduled payment is not made or if the homeowner sells the property. Most mortgage contracts include this clause.

Addendum: An addendum is something added. In real estate, the main addendum is a page added to the sales contract. Addendums should by initialed by all concerned parties.

Appurtenances: Whatever is annexed to the land or used with it that will pass to the buyer. A garage or garden shed is an appurtenance.

Assessed Valuation: An evaluation of property by an agency of the government for taxation purposes.

Assessment: A tax or charge levied on a property by a taxing authority to pay for improvements such as sidewalks, streets, and sewers.

Chattel: Personal property or items such as furniture, appliances, and lighting fixtures, which are not permanently affixed to the home being sold.

Cloud on the Title: A *cloud on the title* means there is a defect in the title that may affect the owner's ability to market his or her property. It could be a lien, a claim, or a judgment. In almost all cases, a cloud on the title would mean a postponement of the closing until it can be resolved by the seller. In rare cases, a buyer has offered to clear the lien. However, the lender will likely have reservations and refuse to go through with the sale until all problems have been resolved.

Easement: An access or right of way. The right of one party to cross or use the property for some specified purpose. For example, water, sewage, and utility suppliers often hold an easement across private property.

Prospectus: A document, sometimes referred to as an offering plan, prepared by condominium and cooperative sponsors, detailing ownership on the development, location, prices, and layouts of the units; procedures to purchase; and other information on how the property is to be run.

Redlining: Alleged practice of some lending institutions involving their refusal to make loans on properties they deem to be bad risks.

Report of Title: A document required before title insurance can be issued.

Right of Survivorship: This is granted to owners who purchase property as "joint owners." The document stipulates that one gets full rights and becomes sole owner of the property on the death of the other.

To Convey the Property: To convey simply means to transfer the property from one to another. The document by which the title is transferred is called the conveyance.

Waiver: This is a document that surrenders some right, claim, or prerogative.

Q: What should I do after the closing?

A: You have made it through the closing, the house is yours, but now it's time to think about moving. Do not become overwhelmed; you can get through this. One of the first things you need to do is to remove your name from the utilities, telephone, cable, newspaper service, and trash service at your former address. Then call the utility services to confirm the move-in date and request that everything be either connected or turned over to your name. If the move requires that your children change schools, be sure to notify the schools and pick up transfer papers. Changing the locks at the new house should be on your list of things to do.

One last thing you should do is celebrate. Your dream has come true; the property now belongs to you. Don't become weighed down with the idea of getting things perfect right way. It's going to take you a while to unpack, to arrange your furniture, and to decorate. It may even take a while before the house really starts feeling . . . right. Sometimes it may take changing the color scheme or buying some new window treatments before you start feeling your own personality coming alive in the rooms. But each time you open that door with your new set of keys, each time you find the right spot for one of your favorite collectables or a framed photograph, your sense of belonging will increase. It won't take long until the house you loved from afar will eventually turn into your home.

The 250 Questions

Part One: Deciding to Purchase

1. To own or rent—which is right for you?
2. Can I afford to buy a home?
3. How much can I afford?
4. How much money will I need to buy a house?
5. How can I begin to budget for buying a house?
6. Saving sounds great, but it would take years—am I the only person who doesn't have an extra $10,000 or $15,000 at my disposal to use as a down payment?
7. Can I use any of the funds in my IRA for the down payment?
8. Can I use any of the funds in my 401K for the down payment?
9. What type of house do I want and need?
10. Where do I want to live?
11. What are the advantages and disadvantages of living in the inner city?
12. What are the advantages and disadvantages of living in the suburbs?
13. What are the advantages and disadvantages of living in the country?
14. What is a seller's market and a buyer's market?
15. Is there an optimum time of the year to shop for a home?
16. Do I need a real estate agent?
17. How do I find a real estate agent?
18. How do I know if the real estate agent is qualified?
19. What is a multiple listing service?
20. Is one agency better than another?
21. If the seller pays the fee of the agent, who does the agent really represent?
22. Do I need more than one agent?
23. What does the term dual agency mean, and why isn't it recommended?
24. What if I just happen to fall in love with one of my agent's listings in which he or she represents the seller?
25. Should the whole family go to look at homes?
26. How many homes should I expect to see in one day?
27. What should I take with me to view homes?

28. How many times is too many times to revisit a home?
29. Can I take pictures or a video of the home so I can review my findings later?
30. What if, after I commit to an agent, I don't feel we are a good match?
31. What should I do if I feel that I'm being excluded from certain neighborhoods?
32. What is the difference between a real estate agent and a broker?
33. What is a buyer's broker?
34. Do I need a buyer's broker?
35. How do I find a buyer's broker?
36. Do I need a lawyer to purchase a home?
37. What does it mean to be preapproved?
38. What is the difference between being preapproved and being prequalified?
39. Should I be preapproved for a home loan?
40. Does it cost anything to be preapproved?
41. If I'm just getting preapproved to start looking for a home, do I really need to be selective of which lender I choose to do the preapproval process?
42. Is my credit good enough to buy a home?
43. How can I check my credit, and do I have to pay for it?
44. What is a credit bureau?
45. If there are three major credit bureaus, will all three reports be the same?
46. What is a credit report and what information does a credit report include?
47. What are the red flags that may prevent me from getting a loan?
48. What if it isn't bad credit holding me back, but rather no credit?
49. How can I start building my credit?
50. How long does it take to build one's credit?
51. Does a credit bureau approve or deny credit?
52. What is a credit risk score?
53. How can a high credit score help me?
54. How long does information stay on my credit report?
55. What is a mortgage report?
56. Who may check my credit report?
57. What if I find something on my credit that is false?
58. If I'm turned down due to my credit by one lender, will I be turned down by all?
59. My lender said I have an A rating; what is this rating and what does it mean?

60. What if I've had credit in the past and paid my bills on time, but it's not showing up on my report?
61. What are some quick steps I can take to improve how my credit appears in the near future?
62. I have good credit but very little money for a down payment—can I buy a house?
63. How do I start to repair bad credit?
64. How long does it take to repair bad credit?
65. I applied for bankruptcy in the past; can I get a home loan?
66. Are there options for me if I really want to buy a house right now but my credit isn't any good?

Part Two: Loan Wisdom

67. What is a mortgage?
68. What is leveraging and why is it important?
69. What factors determine the amount of my monthly mortgage payment?
70. What is included in a monthly mortgage payment?
71. What is equity?
72. What is a loan to value (LTV) ratio and how does it determine the size of my loan?
73. What are points?
74. Why is it so important to shop for a lender? Aren't all lenders the same?
75. When is really the right time to shop for a loan?
76. How do I start to shop for lenders?
77. What do I look for in a lender?
78. What should I bring with me when I apply for a loan?
79. Can I get information on mortgages online?
80. What can I learn on a no-loan site, and what are the Web addresses?
81. Can I really get approved for a loan on the Internet?
82. Are all online mortgage sites the same?
83. What should I know before completing an online mortgage?
84. What is the best way to compare loan terms between lenders, both online and off?
85. I've been preapproved by a lender; is it too late to shop for the best loan now?
86. How long does it take to be preapproved for a loan?
87. What is RESPA?
88. Where can I get a copy of RESPA?
89. What is a good-faith estimate?
90. How can I protect myself against loan fraud?

91. What is an amortization table?
92. Exactly what is APR?
93. Will the best APR be the lowest?
94. So, should I shop for a loan comparing APRs, or should I be comparing interest rates?
95. Exactly how does the interest rate factor into securing a mortgage loan?
96. What causes interest rates to change constantly?
97. How do I decide which loan will be best for me?
98. Are there special mortgages for first-time homebuyers?
99. What is a conventional loan?
100. What are the advantages of opting for a fifteen-year loan versus the traditional thirty-year loan?
101. What is a fixed-rate loan?
102. What are the advantages and disadvantages of a fixed-rate loan?
103. If I go with a fixed rate, what happens if interest rates decrease?
104. What is a balloon mortgage?
105. When should I consider a balloon mortgage and when is it not a good idea?
106. What is an adjustable-rate mortgage?
107. What makes an ARM's interest rate go up and down?
108. What is an index, and is one index better than another?
109. What are the advantages and disadvantages of an ARM mortgage?
110. What are the questions I should ask the loan officer before choosing an ARM?
111. What is an adjustable-rate cap?
112. What is an adjustment interval, and how soon and how often does it fluctuate?
113. What are hybrid loans?
114. What are low-doc or no-doc loans?
115. What are prepayment penalties?
116. Is the lowest interest rate always the best?
117. What is an escrow account and do I need one?
118. What is private mortgage insurance (PMI)?
119. How much does PMI cost?
120. Is there any way to avoid paying PMI?
121. Because of my lack of credit, I was told I might need a cosigner— exactly what is a cosigner?
122. What is the U.S. Department of Housing and Urban Development?
123. How does HUD assist homebuyers and homeowners?
124. How can I get listings of HUD homes for sale?

125. If I am interested in a HUD home, what do I do?
126. I am a teacher and I've heard of the program TND (Teacher Next Door). What is it?
127. Can I qualify to participate in the TND program?
128. How is a TND property sold?
129. What is the Officer Next Door program?
130. How can I get more information about HUD and its programs?
131. What is the federal Farmers Home Administration (FmHA) and how can it help me become a homeowner?
132. What is Fannie Mae?
133. Is Freddie Mac the same as Fannie Mae?
134. What is the FHA?
135. Exactly how can FHA help me buy a house?
136. How is the FHA funded?
137. Can I qualify for an FHA loan?
138. Is there a loan limit for FHA loans?
139. What steps are involved in getting an FHA loan?
140. Do I make enough money to qualify for an FHA loan?
141. Is there a debt-to-income ratio for FHA loans?
142. How does the debt-to-income ratio for FHA compare to the debt-to-income ratios of conventional loans?
143. Is there any way to exceed the debt-to-income ratio with FHA loans?
144. Exactly how much of a down payment do I need to get an FHA loan?
145. What kind of financial resources can I use for the down payment and closing costs of an FHA loan?
146. Is FHA generally more flexible than conventional lenders when it comes to reviewing credit history?
147. What are the closing costs with an FHA-insured loan?
148. Can I have my FHA closing costs figured into my loan amount?
149. Can I assume an FHA loan?
150. What is the FHA HELP program?
151. Will I be required to get mortgage insurance with an FHA loan?
152. What is the FHA 203(b) loan?
153. Which FHA program should I look to if I am planning to purchase a fixer-upper?
154. What is a Title 1 loan?
155. What is an energy efficient mortgage (EEM)?
156. What other programs or loan products does FHA offer the consumer?
157. Where can I go to obtain an FHA-insured loan?
158. What is a VA Guaranteed Home Loan?
159. Are all veterans eligible for a VA loan?

160. Am I limited to only one VA loan?
161. Can I build a new home with a VA loan?
162. How much is my VA entitlement?
163. What is my maximum VA loan limit?
164. How do I apply for a VA guaranteed loan?
165. How do I get a Certificate of Eligibility?
166. How does the closing cost of a VA loan compare to that of conventional loans?
167. What is the VA prepurchase counseling?
168. Can I get a VA loan if I have filed for bankruptcy in the last few years?

Part Three: Shopping for a Home

169. How does one evaluate a neighborhood?
170. Where do I look for information on the property tax liability?
171. How many homes should I see before buying one?
172. Does the location of the home and lot placement in the neighborhood make a difference?
173. What other concerns should I have about a neighborhood or an area before I buy?
174. What is a FSBO?
175. Since a FSBO is being sold without the costs of an agency/broker, can't I get more home for my money in a FSBO home?
176. What happens if I find my dream home and it just happens to be a FSBO?
177. How can I find out about FSBOs?
178. Is an older home a better value than a new one?
179. What is a disclosure?
180. How do I know the true value of a home?
181. Should I be concerned about the homeowners association?
182. Does a fixer-upper mean the seller will not pay for any repairs?
183. When a home is referred to as a fixer-upper, how much fixing will it require?
184. What are the advantages of buying a fixer-upper?
185. What are the disadvantages of buying a fixer-upper?
186. What are some special concerns I need to consider, or questions I need to ask, before buying a fixer-upper?
187. What are the most common defects in an older home?
188. If I find something wrong with the house, can I ask the sellers to fix it?
189. What advice is there for homeowners looking to buy a new home?
190. How do I find developments during the preconstruction phase?
191. How can I know if the builder I picked is a good one?

192. What should I look for when walking through a newly built house?
193. What is a punch list?
194. Are there ways to save on buying a home in a new development?
195. What is an attached home, and should I consider purchasing one?
196. Are there special issues I should check out before buying attached housing?
197. I have heard of condominiums going bankrupt and of internal conflicts about maintenance and upkeep causing serious problems for the homeowners; are there warning signs of a problem condominium or cooperative?
198. What is a patio home?
199. Is a seller-purchased warranty a good benefit?
200. When is it time to make an offer on a property?

Part Four: Making an Offer
201. I found the house I want to buy; what's my next step?
202. Should I ask my agent what to offer for the house?
203. Should I have my own appraisal done so I will be sure that I'm not offering too much?
204. I've heard it is reasonable to offer 10 percent less than the asking price—is this true?
205. Can I negotiate the price of a new home?
206. Exactly what is a purchase agreement?
207. What are contingencies and how do they protect me?
208. Can I have too many contingencies?
209. What are some tips for negotiating?
210. What happens when the seller counteroffers?
211. What happens if we can't reach an agreement?
212. What is earnest money?
213. How much earnest money should I set aside and what happens to it if the deal falls through?
214. When is the right time to start shopping for insurance?
215. What other types of insurance should I consider?
216. How do I get the best price for the insurance I need for the new house?
217. Do I need insurance for a condo or co-op?
218. Who pays for the inspection, how much does it cost, and how long does it take?
219. When should the inspection take place?
220. What are the inspector's responsibilities, and what should I know before hiring one?
221. What is the best way to find a home inspector and how do I know if he is reliable?

222. Can a house fail inspection?
223. Should I have a new home inspected?
224. What can I do if the builder hasn't completed some of the smaller items in my home?
225. Can I count on moving into my newly built house when the builder says I can?
226. What are building codes and what happens if a violation is uncovered during the inspection?
227. What is an appraisal?
228. What happens during an appraisal?
229. What happens if the house doesn't appraise for the requested selling price?

Part Five: Closing and Contract Facts

230. What exactly is a closing and what makes up closing costs?
231. Are there fees I should question?
232. Can I get the seller to pay some of my closing costs?
233. What is a "HUD/1" or settlement statement, and why is it considered one of the most important documents to review during closing?
234. I've heard of no-cost mortgages where there are no closing costs; do they exist?
235. Are closing costs negotiable?
236. Are there ways to save on my closing costs?
237. Where does the closing take place?
238. What can I expect to happen on closing day?
239. What should I do before closing?
240. What do I do if I find some of the contingencies in my purchasing agreement have not been met?
241. How do I handle a late closing?
242. What will I need to bring to the closing?
243. What can I expect to get at the closing?
244. Who needs to be at the closing?
245. Can I move into the new house before closing?
246. What if the seller does not want to move until after the closing?
247. What is a title search and who pays for it?
248. What is title insurance?
249. Are there other terms that I might need to know to get me through the closing process?
250. What should I do after the closing?

Index

About the Author

In Christie Craig's twenty-year career as a columnist, writer, and photo journalist, she's attained more than 700 national magazine credits and has published one fictional novel and one novelette. A firm believer in the age-old adage "Home is where the heart is," she lives in Houston, Texas.